Betty Crocker's
PARTIES
for Children

Betty Crocker's

by LOIS M. FREEMAN

illustrated by JUDY and BARRY MARTIN

PARTIES
for Children

Golden Press New York

We're Having A POW-WOW!

DEAR PARTY GIVER,

Children love parties—they are such eager and enthusiastic guests. And they learn to be good hosts and hostesses, too, when you let them help you plan parties for their friends.

But successful parties don't just "happen." They require careful thought and planning in advance. What invitations and decorations shall we use? What games shall we play? What favors shall we give? And, very important at any party, what shall we serve to eat?

Haven't you often wished for a really complete party guide to answer all these questions and more? Well, here it is: a new book to add to your Library of Betty Crocker Cook Books.

To collaborate with us on writing it, we engaged the services of a well-known authority on party counseling and child psychology, Lois M. Freeman.

A professional children's party counselor for eighteen years, Miss Freeman has arranged more than 5,000 parties. Many summers as a camp counselor and years of teaching have given her keen insight into the world of children. Now Assistant Principal of a New York City elementary school, she has a master's degree in school psychology—and she is still giving parties for children!

We believe you will find this colorful, picture-filled book brimful of imaginative ideas and good advice to help you entertain young guests of every age group, 5 through 11.

Miss Freeman's instructions for more than 150 games and activities are the perfect solution to your problem of "What to do at the party." Our Party Planner menus and recipes have been carefully chosen to carry out special party themes, and all recipes have been tested in our Kitchens so that you can be sure of serving the foods children really enjoy.

Plan to use this book for camp and school activities, too. The games will provide hours of fun for Brownie and Cub Scout troops, for rainy days indoors, and for summer playtime. There are also suggestions for adapting party ideas for handicapped children.

Next time you're planning a children's party, reach for this book. You'll enjoy hearing the boys and girls exclaim that "the best parties happen at your house."

Cordially,

Betty Crocker

Contents

How to Make a Tracing

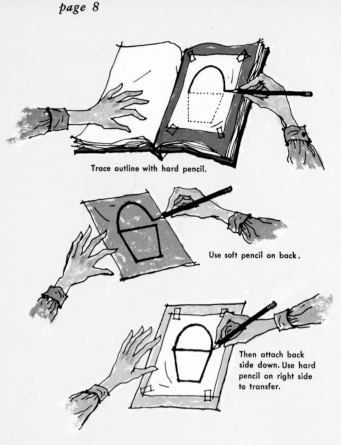

Trace outline with hard pencil.

Use soft pencil on back.

Then attach back side down. Use hard pencil on right side to transfer.

It will help you to use the patterns in this book if you know how to make a tracing. While it is best to use tracing paper, tissue paper may be used instead.

1. Lay the tracing paper over the pattern to be traced. Use masking tape or cellophane tape to attach it to the page on which the desired pattern appears.

2. Trace around the outline of the pattern with a sharp pencil. Remove the tracing paper by snipping the tape with scissors.

3. To transfer the pattern to a white or light-colored surface, go over the back of the tracing paper with a soft pencil. Then tape or pin the tracing (back side down) to the surface on which you wish the transferred pattern to appear. Go over the lines on the right side of the tracing with a hard pencil.

4. To transfer the pattern to a dark-colored surface, use chalk to go over the back of the tracing. Place tracing in position and go over the lines on the right side with a hard pencil.

How to Enlarge
and Reduce Patterns

By following these directions, you will be able to enlarge or reduce any pattern in this book.

TO ENLARGE: Make a tracing of the pattern you plan to use. Then mark off this tracing with squares —¼ inch for small designs, ½ or 1 inch for larger designs.

If you want the pattern to be twice as large, make a copy sheet out of a second sheet of tracing paper by marking it off with squares that are twice as large as those on your original tracing. (For instance, you may have used ½-inch squares to mark off your original tracing. You will then mark off your copy sheet with 1-inch squares.)

Place these two sheets next to each other and carefully reproduce the lines of the original tracing on the copy sheet. If you draw in the lines one square at a time, you will find it is quite easy to enlarge the pattern almost identically.

TO REDUCE: Simply reverse the method used for enlarging designs. For instance, mark off your original tracing with 1-inch squares and your copy sheet with ½-inch squares.

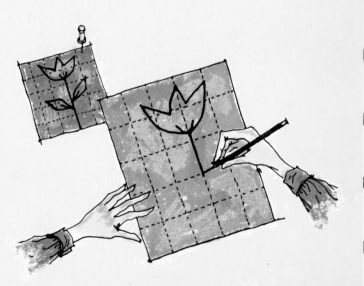

Why Have a Party?

The answer to the above question may be simply, "To have fun!" Even though you probably agree with that, you may find additional answers. During every moment of a child's day he is learning something. He doesn't have to wait until he grows up before putting into practice some of the skills and ideas learned through play. Yet as an adult, he will also need to know how to work and play with other people, how to entertain, and how to be a guest. He will be able to do all of these things more easily if as a child he has been exposed to social gatherings where his experiences were pleasant and meaningful.

Thus, in addition to being fun, your child's party can be an invaluable learning situation. Shy or insecure children can be the focus of quiet attention at their own parties. Knowledge beforehand of just what will take place at the party will help this child to gain confidence as a young host or hostess. On the other hand, more exuberant youngsters will find outlets for their leadership abilities and less need to bluster and swagger when they are, quite legitimately, the center of attraction for a day.

So perhaps the answer to the above question should be twofold: "To have fun and to learn while doing."

Whether you are planning your first party or your twenty-fifth, the wealth of information contained in this book will assure you of the best parties you have ever given.

On pages 10-17, all of the PRELIMINARY stages of a party are discussed. You will find answers to such questions as: Where shall we hold the party? How long should it last? How many children should we invite? What about a theme? You will also find hints for a number of ways in which your child can help to plan and prepare for his party.

All the necessary PREPARATIONS for a party are covered on pages 18-25. Suggestions are included for sending out invitations, and directions and patterns for making 12 original invitations are given. Decorations for the party, suitable prizes, and just-right refreshments are also suggested. (On pages 153-166 you will find *complete* menus with recipes and suggested games to help you fit your party to any special occasion.)

The very large section of the book found on pages 26-149 covers perhaps the most important part of all, the PROGRAM, or entertainment. Suggestions are given for planning such activities as movies, magic shows, puppet shows, and trips. Over 150 games are described in detail, with the number of players needed and the age range given for each game. Groups of games have been pre-selected from this section as ideal party programs for various ages.

The PARTY-GIVER'S CHECK LIST on page 150-151 shows at a glance what steps are necessary for planning a successful party.

How Can Your Child Help?

You are going to have a party, either because your child has asked for one or because you have decided that it would be a good idea. From this point on, communication between you and your child is most important. He cannot just bring his friends home on the afternoon of his birthday to find you unprepared. And you will find that you cannot go very far in planning a party without consulting him.

A surprise party given for an elementary school child robs him of the pleasure of anticipation. And further, he misses out on the opportunity for the social learning associated with making and carrying out his own plans. Although it might be easier for you to make your plans and purchases alone, such decisions rightly belong to the young host or hostess, within the framework of your guidance.

Find out what kind of party your child has in mind. He may want it to be exactly like every other party he has attended in the past year. Or he may want to try something different.

Consult the Party-Giver's Check List on pages 150-151 to see at what times your child can be particularly helpful. Many young children are not interested in all the details of each stage of planning. They usually have decided opinions, however, on who should come to their party. They will more than likely enjoy helping you make the invitations and decorations. And when it comes time to choose the prizes and favors, they will probably go shopping with you willingly.

An older child is apt to have very definite ideas about the theme of the party, who should be invited, what games should be played, what refreshments should be served, and so forth. He may want to take a very active part during the preparatory stages of the party, assuming full responsibility for the invitations, decorations, and "take-home" bags.

The older child will probably enjoy selecting the favors and prizes without you. Discuss with him beforehand what sum of money can be spent, and then leave the rest up to him. If the things he brings home are not what you would have chosen, remember—it's his party! His friends will be sure to tell him whether or not they approve of his selections.

You may want to act out ahead of time some of the new situations which a young child will encounter. Show him how to greet guests, how to accept presents graciously, how to cut the cake, and how to say good-by. Act out these situations on several occasions before the actual party, and have the child play a different role each time. Then, on the day of the party, he will have some idea of what is expected of him in his role as the young host.

If this is to be an enjoyable event for both of you, with increased knowledge of social graces for your child, you can see that the planning and preparation for your party must be a two-way affair.

Where Shall We Hold the Party?

A child's own home is first choice for the place in which to hold the party. Here the child feels most secure, knows where everything is, and can be a natural host or hostess. If, however, there is illness in the family or a new baby, the party might be held at the home of a close relative.

Many parents are hesitant about holding children's parties in their homes. Some are deterred by lack of space. However, it is possible to play games in a cleared area only six by nine feet. And refreshments need not always mean an elaborately set party table with a place for each child.

Today, many homes contain recreation rooms or family rooms. With spillproof floors and washable furniture coverings, these rooms make ideal party settings. Such rooms are usually laid out so that refreshments and games can all take place within the one room.

If a party must be held in the living room, put away any valuable accessories, for accidents do happen. Many of the games in this book can be played with the children seated in a circle on the floor, so you need not be overly concerned about the children climbing on your good living room furniture.

If the party is held in the child's room, it is a good idea to see that all toys are put away beforehand. Since young children are easily distracted by toys, it will be difficult to get their cooperation for the party games you have planned unless this has been done.

Do not overlook the possibility of a party in the backyard, especially in the warmer months. However, an outdoor party should never be planned without making alternate provisions, in detail, in case of inclement weather. It might be wiser to plan an indoor party, with two or three activities which could be conducted outside if the weather cooperates.

Some parents do not wish to hold parties in their homes because they do not feel capable of coping with a large group of children. For this reason, it is a good idea to have at least one other person to help you—another adult or a reliable teen-ager. If you have to be out of the room to set up another game or to prepare the refreshments, then this person is available to supervise the children. Wherever the children play, however, they should be free from the scrutiny of too many adult observers.

No matter where in the home the party is held, it is important that an atmosphere of warmth and friendliness should prevail from the first guest's arrival until the last good-by.

When Should We Have the Party?

Most children's parties are birthday parties. Becoming a year older is an important event in the life of a child, to be shared with relatives when he is very young and certain to be celebrated in some manner as he grows older. When a child reaches kindergarten age, has his own friends, and understands participation in a group, he is ready for his very own party.

This party may be scheduled for the actual day of his birthday, or the week end preceding or following that day. A child who is not yet in school or whose birthday falls on a non-school day will most likely have his party on the actual date of his birthday.

However, it is difficult to hold a party on a school day. The children are tired after a full day's work at school. They need an active, outdoor, less organized program than that which makes for a successful party. If you decide to have a group come directly from school, you do solve the problem of late-comers, but you are apt to create a far greater problem. The group may descend on you *en masse* with a "school's out, now we can make merry" attitude.

If there is school the next day, you may also run the risk of interfering with early bedtimes for younger children or homework for the older ones. Explain all of these reasons to your child and try to select a day close to his birthday on which there is no school.

Avoid Sundays, if possible. Sundays attract relatives. If the party must be held on a Sunday, be sure to inform everyone that this is a children's party.

The child whose birthday occurs during the summer may find that his friends are not going to be home at the time of his birthday, or he himself may be away on vacation. In this case he may wish to plan a party a month earlier or later than his actual birthday, so as not to miss out on a party altogether. If, on the other hand, most of his friends stay close to home in the summertime, it is actually an ideal time for a party. Parties can be held in the backyard, at the beach, or at a picnic area. A whole new group of activities can be planned which are not possible during the rest of the year.

Children who move to a new neighborhood or start classes in a new school may find their places in the group more easily if their new acquaintances are invited to a party. Before you plan such a party, check to see what kinds of parties are usual for this new circle of friends. Do not introduce too many different ideas too suddenly.

The time element of a party is as important as the day of a party. A late party causes the children to wait all day before it begins. And a too-early party may interfere with afternoon naps for some younger children.

Children do not take long to eat at a party. When planning the time for refreshments, allow just 20 minutes for ice cream and cake, 30 minutes for a simple luncheon or supper, and about 45 minutes for a dinner party.

MORNING PARTIES Little children are at their best in the morning. An unusual party for five-year-olds might be scheduled from 10:30 a.m. until 12:30 p.m., with lunch served at noon.

LUNCHEON PARTIES for six- to 11-year-olds should last about three hours. Consult the chart for suggested times. Refreshments should, of course, be served first. Be sure that the parents are aware of the going-home time. Otherwise the party is apt to drag on almost to suppertime!

AFTERNOON PARTIES, at which ice cream and cake are served rather than a full meal, should be planned for about 2 to 2½ hours. Refreshments should be served as soon as all the guests have arrived so as not to interfere with appetites for supper.

SUPPER PARTIES should also be planned to last for about 2 to 2½ hours. Serve supper during the last half hour. With proper timing, the children should be just finishing their supper as their parents are arriving to pick them up. The most carefully planned party can disintegrate completely if children finish early and are not immediately provided with something more to do. It might be wise, therefore, to keep in mind a simple guessing game in case just such an emergency arises.

EVENING PARTIES Older children may clamor for an evening party. If all of the children are assured of transportation home, you might plan a party which would begin at 6 p.m. with a simple dinner. Such a party may last for 2½ to 3 hours.

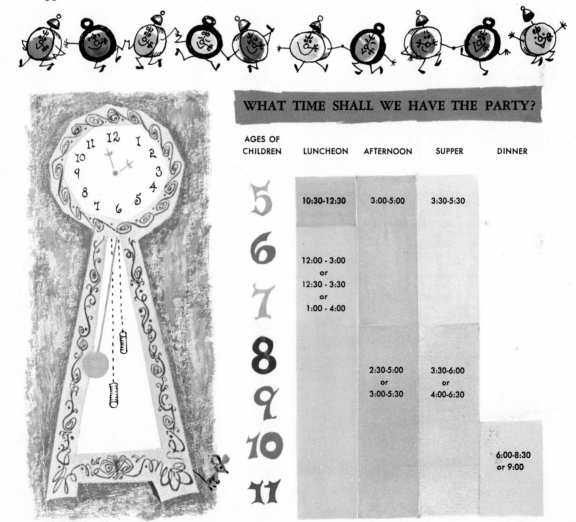

WHAT TIME SHALL WE HAVE THE PARTY?

AGES OF CHILDREN	LUNCHEON	AFTERNOON	SUPPER	DINNER
5	10:30-12:30	3:00-5:00	3:30-5:30	
6	12:00 - 3:00 or 12:30 - 3:30 or 1:00 - 4:00			
7				
8		2:30-5:00 or 3:00-5:30	3:30-6:00 or 4:00-6:30	
9				
10				6:00-8:30 or 9:00
11				

????? Whom Shall We Invite? ?????

The guest list for your party is determined by two important factors: the age of your child and the size of your home. Generally speaking, the older the child, the larger the guest list. However, if you invite too many children, there will be so much noise and confusion that it will be difficult to play the games successfully. If you invite just a few children and some of them cannot make it at the last minute, it will not seem like a party at all.

The chart on page 15 will serve as a guide when considering how many children to invite.

As you will note, five- and six-year-olds are usually friendly with children of both sexes, and boys and girls will play happily together. However, between the ages of seven and 11, parties are generally more successful when limited to either boys or girls. It is easier to plan activities which appeal to the entire group. Although boys and girls in this age group often enjoy the same games, they play them differently.

Very often the question arises, "Should I invite my child's whole class to the party?" If the class has only a dozen members, this is possible. Most classes are larger, however, and there may also be a few guests who are not members of this class. Do not try to pare down your guest list by inviting all but one or two members of such a class. These few children will be sure to feel hurt and left out. Instead, if you are faced with the problem of a large class, invite only those children who are closest to your child.

If possible, the guests should be within a few months or a year of the party child's age. If the child has only one or two brothers or sisters, they may also attend the party. Watch, however, that a baby does not draw attention away from the guest of honor, or that an older child's help does not become interference.

Children in the same family may have birthdays in the same month, or even in the same week. It may seem difficult, but try to give each child a separate party on a separate day. Even though they may be close in age, they are bound to have different friends and interests. Twins may wish to have one party. However, if they are in different classes and play with different children, they may wish to hold two parties on the same day but in different rooms.

Infrequently seen cousins or children of parents' friends need not be invited to a party. Adults in general should not be invited to a children's party. You may wish to have one or two adults present to help you. But if a number of relatives insist on coming, there should be a separate family celebration.

Many parents feel obliged to invite the parents of their child's guests to "Come back later for coffee and cake." This is unnecessary hospitality. Invite these parents for a party of their own at another time. Chances are, when they return to pick up their children, the children will be really ready to go home and will resent having to wait while the adults prolong the party.

Consult with your child on whom he wants to come to his party. With a little give-and-take on his part and yours, you will be sure to come up with just the right guest list for the kind of party you have in mind.

Karen   Charles   Ed   Selma   Fred & Frank   Gloria   Bruno

HOW MANY GUESTS SHALL WE INVITE?

AGES OF CHILDREN	INVITE BETWEEN	IDEAL NO. OF GUESTS	BOYS OR GIRLS	
5 to 6 Years	8 and 12	10		AND
7 to 8 Years	12 and 18	12	ALL	or ALL
9 to 11 Years	10 and 15	15	ALL	or ALL

What About Presents?

Many children are inclined to feel that presents are the most important part of their party. There is something exciting about the idea of receiving gifts—even most adults will attest to this. But it is not pleasant to watch a birthday child plunge into the opening of his presents without so much as a word of greeting or thank-you to his guests.

Play "Pretend Party" with your child several times before his party so that he will know just how to greet his guests at the door. If the guest offers him a present, show him how to say "thank you" graciously.

Decide beforehand where your child should place his presents and at what point in the party he will open them. A good time to open gifts is just before the actual party activities begin—or after the refreshments have been served. You might suggest that your child open his presents as soon as he has received two or three. Most youngsters soon lose interest in a long unwrapping ceremony. Be sure to see that the unwrapped gifts are put aside immediately. Provide a carton or wastepaper basket for discarded wrappings.

Children should know what is inside the gaily wrapped packages they bring to a party. Even the youngest guests will enjoy selecting presents for their friends. If a child is unable to attend a party at the last minute, his present should be delivered for him, or given to the party child as soon after the party as possible.

Presents can be a costly item throughout the year for the parents of a child who is invited to many parties. Relatives will often choose to give items of clothing or more expensive toys for which a child has expressed a preference. Young guests should choose less elaborate presents; often a maximum amount to be spent can be set up by a group of parents. Two dollars would certainly be more than adequate, and something the child would really like to have might cost considerably less.

Children are never too young to send thank-you notes. Younger ones may dictate their notes, but they will enjoy stamping and mailing them themselves. Older children, with a little prompting on your part, can take full responsibility for their own notes.

Encourage your child to take stock of his possessions after an occasion such as a birthday party. With so many new toys at his disposal, it would be an ideal time to clean out those things which no longer interest him. Many organizations are happy to receive cast-off toys for repair and redistribution.

We're having a POW-WOW

ALL ABOARD

PARTY

What ✳ · ✳ *About* *a Theme?*

Most young children prefer an old-fashioned, typical birthday party. However, sometimes it is fun to select a special theme for the party around which you can coordinate the invitations, decorations, and even the games. After several years of playing the same games, children will probably welcome some changes, even if they are just variations in the colors or objects used in the games.

The old favorite Pin the Tail on the Donkey (page 40) can become—with the aid of an old pillow slip and some crayons—Pin the Cow in the Bed, Pin the Dog in the Doghouse, Pin the Button on the Clown, or Pin the Bell on the Christmas Tree.

Chip Change (page 130) may be played with

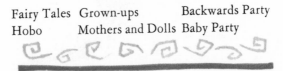

SEASONAL THEMES

January: New Year's Day, Wintertime
February: Lincoln's Birthday, Valentine's Day,
 Washington's Birthday
March: St. Patrick's Day, Springtime
April: April Fool's Day, Easter, Circus
May: Memorial Day
June: Summertime, Graduation
July: Fourth of July, Beach
August: Picnic
September: Back-to-School
October: Columbus Day, Autumn, Halloween
November: Election Day, Book Week,
 Thanksgiving
December: Christmas

BIRD, BEAST, AND FISH THEMES

Horses	Farm Animals	Creatures of the Sea
Pets	Wild Animals	Birds Insects

TRAVEL THEMES

European	Oriental	African
Arctic	Hawaiian	Tropical

TRANSPORTATION THEMES

Ship	Airplane	Trailer
Train	Bus	Space

SPORTS THEMES

Baseball	Football	Winter Sports
Tennis	Basketball	Summer Sports

TV THEMES

Quiz Program	Cowboy
Detective or Mystery	Indian

OTHER THEMES

Fairy Tales	Grown-ups	Backwards Party
Hobo	Mothers and Dolls	Baby Party

chips made to tie in with holiday colors. Try pink, green, and yellow for Easter; orange, black, and yellow for Halloween; red, green, and white for Christmas.

Tracing Stars (page 100) can be varied by tracing pumpkins for Halloween; bells for Christmas or New Year's; hearts for Valentine's Day; bunnies for Easter.

Grandmother's Club (page 51) could be called Witch's Club, Santa's Club, or Bunny Rabbit's Club to tie in with a seasonal or holiday theme.

The patterns given on the following pages can be used to make the invitations pictured above. Many of the invitations tie in directly with the themes suggested here and on pages 154-165.

A number of these themes lend themselves to a costume party: April Fool, Halloween, Circus, Book Week, Cowboy, Hobo, Backwards Party.

Shall We Make the Invitations?

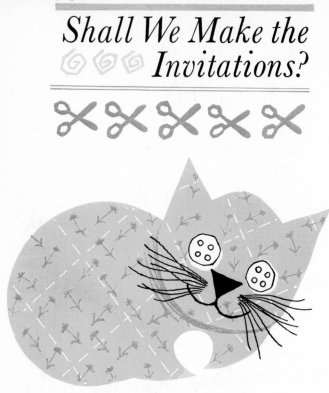

The inside of the invitations should include this information.

> You are invited to a
>
> _____
> (occasion)
> _____
> on _____ _____
>   (day)   (date)
>
> The party will start at
> _____
>
> The party will end at
> _____
>
> (Lunch, supper, refreshments)   will be
>
> served at
> _____
>
> The party will be at _____
>   (child's name)
> _____
>   (address)
>
> _____
>   (phone no.)
>
> Please reply

If the party is a very informal one, given on short notice, the guests may be invited over the telephone. However, sending a gay invitation through the mail establishes an air of festivity about your child's party right from the start. Written invitations will also insure against mistakes in date or time.

If special dress is to be worn (play clothes or costumes), be sure to mention this also.

Invitations should be mailed about 10 days before the party. If they are sent out too early, the date might be forgotten. If the guests receive too short notice, some might not be able to make the party.

Sometimes a child becomes ill on the day of his party. The party will have to be postponed, of course, but need not be canceled entirely. Telephone the guests at once to make a new date for the party, about two weeks hence. If the illness is one which runs its course through the entire family, the party can still be held, even if it is six weeks later. About the only thing that won't keep is the cake!

A number of attractive commercially printed invitations are now on the market. However, your child might enjoy making his own. The gay invitation ideas pictured on pages 16-17 are easy to assemble and require only a few basic supplies: colored construction paper, scissors, crayons, sponge, glue, and poster paints. Patterns and directions for making these invitations are given here and on pages 20-21. Among the dozen, your child will be sure to find one to carry out the theme of his party.

CALICO CAT Use the cat pattern on this page and transfer to a flowered material. Cut out the head and body as two separate pieces. Mount on sheets of paper, 6 x 8 inches, folded in half crosswise. Glue on tiny button eyes, a black paper nose, and black thread whiskers. With crayon, add an oval rug. Print "Come to a Pet Party!"

BASEBALL MITT Cut sheets of yellow paper, 6 x 8 inches—one for each invitation. Fold in half crosswise. Use the mitt pattern on page 19 and cut out of brown paper. Using a half dollar, trace and cut the balls out of white paper. Mount a ball and mitt on the front of each card. Add stitching lines with pencil or crayon. Print "It's Going to Be a Double-Header!"

BLUE-HAIRED WITCH Cut sheets of orange paper, 6 x 8 inches—one for each invitation. Use the witch pattern on this page. Cut the face out of blue paper, the hat out of black. Mount on the orange cards. Glue strands of blue-wool hair under the hat. With crayon, add a brim, eyes, eyebrows, nose, and mouth. Print the Halloween party information on the inside.

CIRCUS BALLOONS Cut sheets of blue construction paper, 6 x 8 inches—one for each invitation. Fold in half crosswise. Use the balloon pattern at the right and transfer it to the top half of each card. Using a quarter as a pattern, trace and cut out different colored balloons for each card. Glue them in place. When dry, cut out around the outline of the balloons at the top of the card, if desired. With pencil or ink, draw in the strings. Add "It's a Party!"

BACKWARDS PARTY Cut sheets of green paper, 6 x 8 inches—one for each invitation. Fold in half crosswise. Use the pattern letters P A R T Y just as they appear below. Cut them out of different colored papers. Glue them, *backwards,* on the front of the invitation. Add "Come to a."

CHRISTMAS TREE Cut sheets of white paper, 4 x 12 inches—one for each invitation. Fold in half crosswise. Use an ordinary household sponge to print the tree. For a stencil, cut a piece of typing paper just slightly larger than the size of the sponge. Cut out a triangle in the middle of the stencil. Wet stencil and sponge. Dip sponge into saucer containing green poster paint. Place sponge down on stencil (stencil remains adhered to sponge during printing). Print as many invitations as you can before sponge dries out. Remove stencil from sponge. Redip sponge in paint, replace on stencil, and continue printing.

For ornaments, dip tip of pencil eraser in red poster paint and print directly on card. Glue on tub cut out of red paper.

(Continued on page 20)

Enlarge patterns by following the directions on page 8.

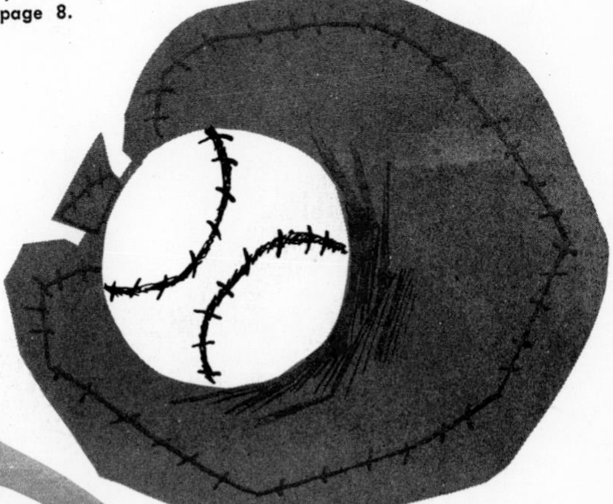

INVITATIONS
(Continued)

Enlarge patterns by following the directions on page 8.

We're having a pow-wow!

ALL ABOARD

For the party train! At Bobby's house on Saturday afternoon, from three till six o'clock

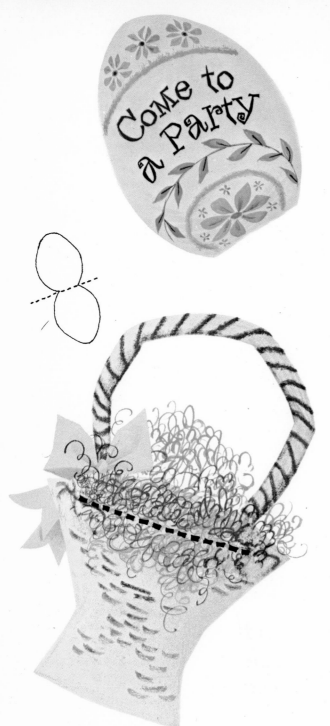

PARTY TRAIN Using the pattern on page 20, trace and cut out of yellow paper one train for each invitation. Cut smokestacks, wheels, headlights, and cab windows out of colored papers and glue in place. Use coins for the wheel patterns. Print "All Aboard!" on the engine and the party information on the boxcar. Fold back the second car to fit the invitation in the envelope.

BEACH PARTY Cut sheets of white paper, 6 x 8 inches—one for each invitation. Fold in half crosswise. Using the patterns given here, trace and cut out one red pail and one blue shovel for each card. Spread rubber cement over the bottom half of each card, and sprinkle with sand. Add a few tiny shells, if you like. Glue pail and shovel in place. Add handle and stripe with crayons.

SKATING MITTENS Your child can make his own mitten pattern by tracing around his hand. Cut two mittens for each invitation out of colored paper. Decorate with crayons. Print "Come to a Skating Party!" on one mitten, and put the party information on the second mitten. Join them with a length of wool stapled to the cuff of each mitten.

EASTER BASKET Using the patterns given here, trace and cut out of colored paper one basket for each invitation. Place the egg pattern on a folded sheet of paper, with one end on the fold. Decorate the outside of the egg with crayon and add "Come to a Party!" Put the party information on the inside of the egg. Cut a slit in the basket and slip the egg into it. If you wish, glue some artificial grass around the slit to make a soft "nest" for the egg.

INDIAN TEPEE Use tepee pattern on page 20. Transfer to folded sheets of tan paper, with the left side of the tepee on the fold. Cut out one for each invitation. With crayons, add Indian designs, and print "We're Having a Pow-wow!" Tape broom straws to the back of the tepees for the poles.

SPRING FLOWERS Cut sheets of white paper, 8 x 8 inches—one for each invitation. Using the patterns given here, trace and cut out one large pink tulip, two purple tulips, and one orange tulip for each card. Place the large tulip pattern on a folded sheet, with the left side of the flower on the fold. Print "It's Spring! It's a Party!" on the inside of the pink tulip. Mount the flowers on the cards (glue one purple tulip on the inside). Add stems and leaves with green crayon.

What About Decorations?

A few simple decorations will add immeasurably to the festivity of a party. Too gaudy an array, however, will only confuse young children. It is wise to confine their decorations to a cluster of balloons (one for each guest, plus extras for breakage) and a colorful table setting, without too much on it.

A slightly older child may wish to do some of the decorating himself, to carry out the theme he has chosen. Certain games can also double as decorations. For instance, for a circus theme, be sure to use the clown described under Cotton Ball Toss (page 62). In another corner hang a variation of Pin the Tail on the Donkey (page 40) to suggest more circus atmosphere.

Crepe-paper streamers (available in any variety store) and dozens of balloons clinging to the walls by means of static electricity automatically say, "There's going to be a party!"

TABLE DECORATIONS AND FAVORS Plan to set the table the morning of the party. Use a paper tablecloth (with plastic underneath to protect your table) and paper napkins, plates, and cups. These come in assorted pastel colors. They can also be purchased with floral, Indian, baseball, circus, or birthday motifs, if you prefer. Plastic forks and spoons are colorful time-savers, and may be taken home as souvenirs by the young guests. At each setting include a candy basket with the child's name on it, a paper hat, and perhaps a snapper or noise-maker.

For the centerpiece, you might wish to make a Jack Horner pie. Decorate a round hatbox with crepe paper or colored construction paper, in keeping with the theme of your party. The one shown here has been made into a drum for a Circus Party. Choose a small gift for each child and wrap it in tissue paper. Tie a long ribbon to each gift. Put the gifts in the box, put on the lid, and run one ribbon to each place. At a given signal (choose a time when there are no refreshments on the table!), tell the children to pull their ribbons.

Small gifts to be used as favors can easily be purchased at the toy counter of a variety store. They will cost between 10 and 25 cents each. Dolls' accessories, jacks, tiny puzzles, card games, yo-yos, and sand toys are all good choices. Encourage your child to choose these token gifts for his friends himself.

If you plan to have the birthday cake as the centerpiece, just wrap the favors and place one at each setting. Your child may prefer to wait and give out the favors as "going-home" gifts.

"TAKE-HOME" BAGS With your child's help, prepare a "take-home" bag for each guest. These can be made from brown paper bags, enhanced with crayon or cut-paper decorations. Print each child's name on a bag. A good time to give out these bags is just after the children finish their refreshments. Extra candies, uneaten cupcakes, favors, snappers, and any prizes won during the game period—all of these can be stowed in the "take-home" bags.

Shall We Have Prizes?

Prizes are traditional at parties. With a little effort on your part, they can become secondary in importance if the actual fun of playing the games is emphasized instead.

You will note that a great many of the games in this book do not require prizes. Younger children often play quite happily without expecting to be rewarded with a prize. If prizes *are* given for young children, however, be sure to see that each child receives at least one small prize before the end of the party.

By the age of nine or ten, most children are highly competitive and scrupulously fair. The winners will expect prizes, one for each game won. If one child seems to be on a winning streak, the group may be encouraged to decide to limit the prizes—two to a player. After that, the child who comes in second receives the prize. When many prizes are to be given out, concentrate on providing attractive table favors and rather insignificant prizes.

If a guest seems particularly disturbed about not winning a prize, see if you can't arrange for him to receive a prize for something! Prizes might be given to the girl with the biggest hair ribbon or the boy sporting the most buttons.

Some children are so competitive that they will go to almost any length to win. Should you observe a child who is not playing fairly, quietly let him know that you cannot permit this—although you understand his wanting to win so much.

If you have a mixed age group at a party, the younger children are often at a disadvantage in games requiring reading ability or manual dexterity. Here is one suggestion for providing each child with a prize. At the beginning of the game period, give each child a blank index card, containing only his name. At the close of each game, award a small gummed star to each player just for his participation; 5 stars to the first-place winner; 3 for second place; and one additional star for third place. At the end of the game period have each child total his number of stars. Display an assortment of prizes (unwrapped, this time) containing at least one more than the number of participants. Start with the child having the highest number of stars, and ask each child in turn to choose a prize. In this way, even the lowest scorer has a choice of prizes.

If your child is planning to select the favors for his party, he can select the prizes at the same time. Establish a monetary limit ahead of time so that he will know just how much he can spend on prizes. If you are planning games which involve teams, you will need identical prizes for each member of the winning team—perhaps a large lollipop or candy bar apiece.

Prizes should be wrapped and placed in a box or on a table near the game area. Booby prizes should not be used. They encourage children to depart from the rules, and they may be upsetting to particularly sensitive children.

What About Refreshments?

In the middle of a most interesting game, a young child is apt to ask, "When does the party begin?" For most children, refreshments are synonymous with the word "party."

Refreshments can be served at different times, depending on whether your party is held in the morning, afternoon, or evening. (See page 13.)

Ice cream and cake are standard fare at almost any children's party. However, many young children do not enjoy tackling large pieces of birthday cake. It might be wise to save the birthday cake (after the candles have been blown out) for the family's dessert that evening, and serve the children cupcakes frosted to match the cake.

For any occasion, keep the refreshments simple. Many children do not eat well when they are away from home or faced with all the excitement of a birthday party. Choose familiar foods for younger children. Older children may wish to experiment with more exotic fare. Suggested party menus for various age groups are given here. An exciting array of additional menus, plus recipes, appears on pages 153-166. They have been carefully chosen to carry out special party themes. And all have been tested, of course, so you can be sure of serving refreshments children really enjoy.

Most of the food preparations should be completed before the guests arrive. It is a good idea to have someone free to set out the refreshments while you are busy supervising the games.

Plan to serve the refreshments in a room that is immune to spilled lemonade and melted ice cream. If you do not have enough space to seat the children around a table, you could spread out a blanket on the floor.

One mother whose home boasted a narrow hallway announced that the refreshments would be served in keeping with the airplane theme of the party. Food was arranged on trays, and the guests were seated in two rows down the hall.

"Serve-yourself" style appeals to older children. One sure success is a soda fountain set-up where guests can concoct their own wildest ice-cream dreams. Just set out the ingredients suggested on the menu and watch the fun begin!

OLD-FASHIONED BIRTHDAY PARTY
Birthday Cake or
Cupcakes Topped with Animal Crackers,
Gum Drops, Tiny Marshmallows
Individual Cups of Ice Cream
Pink Lemonade or Soda Pop
Candy Baskets

AIRPLANE MEAL TICKET
Cold Plates consisting of:
Slice of Ham   Slice of Roast Beef
Potato Chips, Radishes, Carrot Sticks
Hot Buttered Rolls or Salt Sticks
Birthday Cake and Ice Cream
Milk

BOXED PICNIC SUPPER
Potato Chips or
Individual Servings of Potato Salad in
Freezer Cartons
Olives, Pickles, Cherry Tomatoes,
Carrot Sticks
Polished Red Apples   Cookies
Pack the above foods in individually deco-
rated shoe boxes or printed cotton scarves.
Supplement with grilled hot dogs or ham-
burgers and cold orangeade at serving time.

ITALIAN SUPPER PARTY
Cocktail Franks served on Toothpicks
Pizzas, made with English Muffins
Antipasto Tray of Raw Vegetables
Ice Cream or Italian Ices
Birthday Cake   Grape Juice

Recipes for Best Birthday Cakes
may be found on page 166.

YOUNG PEOPLE'S LUNCH
Party Sandwiches
(Use cookie cutters to cut bread in shapes.
Spread with peanut butter, cream cheese,
jelly, chicken, ham spread, egg salad.)
Carrot Sticks   Potato Chips
Chocolate or Plain Milk
Birthday Cake   Ice Cream

SERVE-YOURSELF FOUNTAIN
Assorted Syrups: Chocolate, Butterscotch,
Maple, Strawberry, Pineapple, Marshmallow
Assorted Toppings: Cherries, Nuts,
Chocolate Sprinkles, Tiny Marshmallows,
Whipped Cream
Ice Cream in Assorted Flavors
Milk, Assorted Bottled Sodas
Cookies or Cake   Pretzel Sticks

'janie

What Shall We Do at the Party?

Now that you have planned the refreshments and made the decorations, it is time to decide what the children are going to *do* at the party. If everyone is to enjoy the party (and if at the close of the party you are able to say that you would give another party soon again), then certain activities must be planned. Children can be counted on to initiate some games of their own but a whole afternoon of "free play" can result in chaos.

As soon as the guests have arrived, and presents have been inspected or put aside, it is time to do something.

MOVIES With the advent of television, movies have become a less popular form of entertainment at parties. However, children do enjoy movies, particularly cartoons. If you decide to show movies, ask yourself these questions:

1. Do I have the necessary equipment or must I rent it?

2. Is the equipment in perfect working order? Do I have a spare bulb handy?

3. Who will operate the machine?

4. Are the films to be shown ones which the children will really enjoy? (Home movies, unless they happen to include most of the guests, rarely are.)

5. How long a program shall I plan? (About ½ hour maximum.)

Movies are a passive form of entertainment. The children sit and watch, but contribute very little of themselves.

MAGICIANS Professional magicians belong to the Magicians' Union and can be located through the telephone directory of any large city. Their charges may run as high as $25 for a half hour. Before engaging a professional magician, try to learn something about his reputation. He should be genuinely interested in entertaining children, and at such close range he will need to be highly skilled to measure up to the magic shows which the children have seen on television.

You may be fortunate to have a teen-ager in your area who is interested in magic. Perhaps you can arrange for him to give a show. His fees are apt to be much lower and his performance more spontaneous than that of a professional. A magic show should not run any longer than 20 to 45 minutes.

PUPPET SHOWS Professional puppet shows can be an expensive form of entertainment. Often amateur groups are willing to perform for children's parties. The performance might even be designed so that most of the guests at the party could participate. All children love puppets, and many children are quite expert at handling them, especially hand puppets. A puppet show should run for no longer than 20 to 45 minutes.

TRIPS You may wish to arrange a special trip for your young guests. You could plan to take the children to a puppet show, a ball game, or a movie recommended for young people. It might be fun to tour a museum or visit a local factory. You might take the group to the zoo, an amusement park, or an ice skating or roller skating rink.

In warmer weather, a day at the beach or a state park usually means a cook-out party. Be sure that you have arranged in advance for reservation, if needed, of a picnic area and permission to build a fire. A trip of this sort usually depends on good weather. Have ready an alternate plan to present to the children if the weather does not work in your favor.

When planning a trip, keep these few important points in mind:

1. Be sure each parent knows of your plans in detail, especially if they call for swimming, wearing special clothes, or traveling any distance from home.

2. Arrange to have at least one other adult accompany you, even with a very small group. This person may also be able to share the transportation responsibilities.

3. Make as many advance arrangements as you can (purchasing tickets, asking permission to tour a factory, checking on transportation), so that when you arrive with your group, your plans can go ahead smoothly.

GAMES For most parties, a program of assorted games will insure maximum enjoyment and active participation by all children. Lively games can be alternated with quiet ones, and special games can be chosen to hold the interest of even the youngest guests.

The remainder of this book contains pages and pages of games that are suitable for elementary school children. For the most part, these games require very few materials or advance preparation. They encourage the children to use their imaginations and the skills they have developed thus far.

On pages 28-29 you will find groups of games which have been pre-selected for different ages. In addition, the Party-Giver's Check List of Games found on pages 30-33 contains all of the more than 150 games described in this book. At a glance, you will be able to tell what games are particularly suitable for your child's age group.

What Games Shall We Play?

5 YEAR-OLDS

1. Hot, Warm, Cold
2. Dog and Bone
3. Feeding the Elephant
4. Candy Hunt
5. Push Peanut Race
6. Wonder Ball
7. Magic Circles
8. Surprise Package
9. Story

6 YEAR-OLDS

1. Picture Lotto
2. Murder!
3. Stringing Straws
4. Animal Hunt
5. Pig Race
6. Stepping Stones
7. Choosing Colors
8. Shoe Scramble
9. Story

The party-giver needs to consider several points before making a selection of games for the party:

1. How many children have been invited?
2. What are the ages of these children?
3. How many are boys; how many girls?
4. How much space is available for playing these games? Indoors? Outdoors?
5. How much time do we have for games?
6. What games have these children played recently? Sometimes it is good to include a few old favorites, especially if the children are fairly new at party-going.

The games included in this book are divided into ten groups:

A. Games for the Youngest
B. Guessing Games
C. Games of Skill
D. Hunts
E. Races: Elimination and Relay
F. Elimination Contests
G. Games for Older Children
H. Rotative Games
I. Miscellaneous Games
J. Creative Fun

About nine games can be played at a party. On these two pages you will see sample groups of games for various ages. Use the following guide for making your own selections from the Party-Giver's Check List of Games found on pages 30-33.

FIVE-YEAR-OLDS   Choose two games from Groups A and I, one each from Groups C, D, E, and F. This makes a total of eight games. Complete the game period by reading or telling a story.

SIX- AND SEVEN-YEAR-OLDS   Choose one game each from Groups A, B, C, D, E, F, and two from Group I. Round out the game period with a story.

EIGHT-YEAR-OLDS   Choose one game each from Groups B, C, D, E, F, and I. Choose two games from Group G. Complete the game period by reading or telling a story.

NINE- TO ELEVEN-YEAR-OLDS   Choose one each from Groups B, C, D, E, F, and I. In addition, choose two from Group G, or one each from Groups G and H. Finish up with one of the creative activities from Group J.

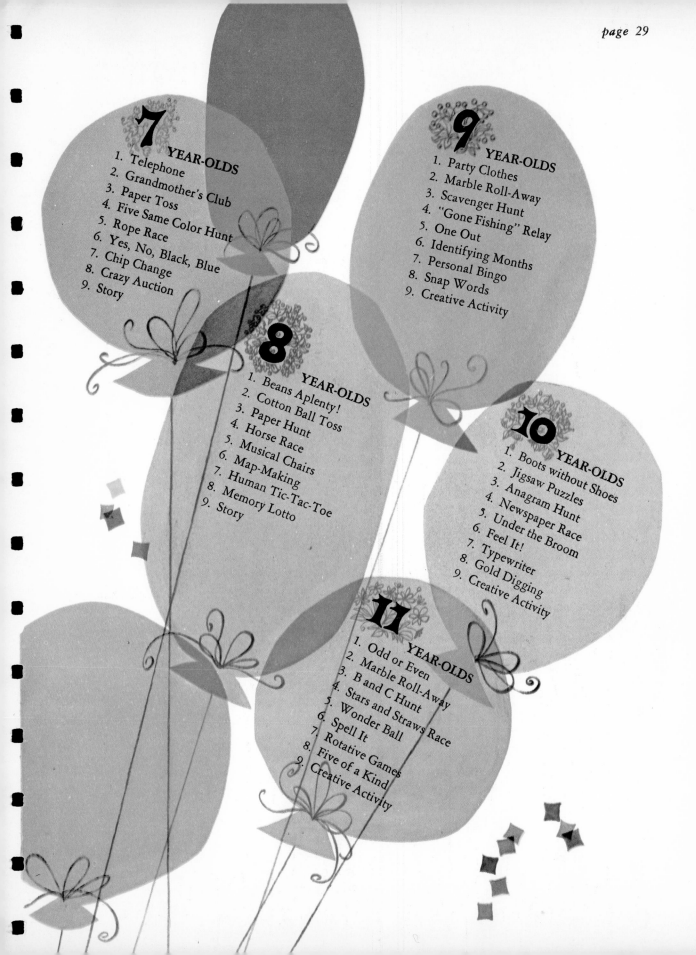

7 YEAR-OLDS

1. Telephone
2. Grandmother's Club
3. Paper Toss
4. Five Same Color Hunt
5. Rope Race
6. Yes, No, Black, Blue
7. Chip Change
8. Crazy Auction
9. Story

9 YEAR-OLDS

1. Party Clothes
2. Marble Roll-Away
3. Scavenger Hunt
4. "Gone Fishing" Relay
5. One Out
6. Identifying Months
7. Personal Bingo
8. Snap Words
9. Creative Activity

8 YEAR-OLDS

1. Beans Aplenty!
2. Cotton Ball Toss
3. Paper Hunt
4. Horse Race
5. Musical Chairs
6. Map-Making
7. Human Tic-Tac-Toe
8. Memory Lotto
9. Story

10 YEAR-OLDS

1. Boots without Shoes
2. Jigsaw Puzzles
3. Anagram Hunt
4. Newspaper Race
5. Under the Broom
6. Feel It!
7. Typewriter
8. Gold Digging
9. Creative Activity

11 YEAR-OLDS

1. Odd or Even
2. Marble Roll-Away
3. B and C Hunt
4. Stars and Straws Race
5. Wonder Ball
6. Spell It
7. Rotative Games
8. Five of a Kind
9. Creative Activity

Party-Giver's Check List of Games

The following list contains the more than 150 games described in this book. They are arranged in the order in which they appear in the book.

For suggestions on how to select a balanced program of games for your child's party, read through the handy guide on page 28.

Games	Page	5 Yrs.	6 Yrs.	7 Yrs.	8 Yrs.	9 Yrs.	10 Yrs.	11 Yrs.
A. GAMES FOR THE YOUNGEST								
Animals Fly	36	*	*					
Beast, Bird, Fish	37	*	*	*				
Button, Button	37	*	*	*				
Picture Lotto	38	*	*	*				
Dog and Bone	39	*	*	*				
Pin the Tail on the Donkey & variations	40	*	*	*	*	*		
Simple Simon	43	*	*	*	*	*		
I See Something	43	*	*	*	*	*		
Fruit Basket	45	*	*	*	*			
Three Up	46	*	*	*	*	*		
Clapping Game	46	*	*	*	*	*	*	
Hot, Warm, Cold	47	*	*	*	*	*	*	
Touch the Spot	48		*	*	*	*		
Telephone	48		*	*	*	*		
Time!	49			*	*	*		
B. GUESSING GAMES								
Murder!	50			*	*	*	*	*
Grandmother's Club	51			*	*	*	*	*
Party Clothes	52				*	*	*	*
Odd or Even	53			*	*	*	*	*
Truth or Consequences	54				*	*	*	*
Twenty Questions	55				*	*	*	*
Beans Aplenty!	56				*	*	*	*
Boots without Shoes	57					*	*	*
Crossed and Uncrossed	57					*	*	*
C. GAMES OF SKILL								
Feeding the Elephant	58	*	*	*	*	*		
Paper Toss	59	*	*	*	*	*		
Jigsaw Puzzles	60		*	*	*	*	*	
Marble Roll-Away	61		*	*	*	*	*	*
Stringing Straws	62	*	*	*	*	*	*	*
Cotton Ball Toss	62		*	*	*	*	*	

Games	Page	5 Yrs.	6 Yrs.	7 Yrs.	8 Yrs.	9 Yrs.	10 Yrs.	11 Yrs.
D. HUNTS								
Candy Hunt	64	*	*	*	*	*	*	*
String Hunt	64	*	*	*	*	*	*	
Animal Hunt	65	*	*	*	*	*		
Scavenger Hunts—								
1 Apt. or House	66			*	*	*	*	*
Apt. Bldg. or 1 Block	68					*	*	*
Outdoors	69					*	*	*
Advertising Slogans Hunt	70					*	*	*
Treasure Hunts—								
Buried Treasure	72			*	*	*	*	*
Sea Shell Hunt	72			*	*	*	*	*
Indoors	73					*	*	*
Five Same Color Hunt	76		*	*	*	*		
Paper Hunt	76		*	*	*	*	*	*
Anagram Hunt	77				*	*	*	*
B and C Hunt	78					*	*	*
String Maze	79			*	*	*	*	*
Card Hunt	79				*	*	*	*
E. RACES—ELIMINATION								
Push Peanut Race	80	*	*	*	*			
Potato Race	81	*	*	*	*	*	*	*
Pig Race	81	*	*	*	*	*		
Rope Race	82	*	*	*	*	*	*	*
Horse Race	82		*	*	*	*	*	*
Stars and Straws Race	83		*	*	*	*	*	*
Tightrope Walking Race	84				*	*	*	*
Egg Race	84			*	*	*	*	*
Scoop Bean Race	85				*	*	*	*
Newspaper Race	85				*	*	*	*
E. RACES—RELAY								
Running Relay	86			*	*	*	*	*
Hopping Relay	86			*	*	*	*	*
Jumping Relay	86			*	*	*	*	*
Skipping Relay	87			*	*	*	*	*
Combination Relay	87			*	*	*	*	*
Overhead Ball Pass Relay	87			*	*	*	*	*

(Continued)

Games	Page	5 Yrs.	6 Yrs.	7 Yrs.	8 Yrs.	9 Yrs.	10 Yrs.	11 Yrs.
E. RACES—RELAY								
Under Leg Ball Pass Relay	87			*	*	*	*	*
Kangaroo Relay	88			*	*	*	*	*
Crawling Relay	88			*	*	*	*	*
Beanbag Exchange Relay	88			*	*	*	*	*
Bowling Relay	89			*	*	*	*	*
Treasure Hunt Relay	89			*	*	*	*	*
Suitcase Relay	89			*	*	*	*	*
Water Carrying Relay	90			*	*	*	*	*
Ball Balancing Relay	90			*	*	*	*	*
Ball and Spoon Relay	90			*	*	*	*	*
Snipping Strips Relay	91			*	*	*	*	*
Rope Relay	91			*	*	*	*	*
Under the Broom Relay	91			*	*	*	*	*
Thread the Needle Relay	92			*	*	*	*	*
"Gone Fishing" Relay	92			*	*	*	*	*
F. ELIMINATION CONTESTS								
Wonder Ball	94	*	*	*	*	*	*	*
Yes, No, Black, Blue	95	*	*	*	*	*		
One Out	95	*	*	*	*	*	*	*
Musical Chairs	96	*	*	*	*	*	*	*
Stepping Stones	97	*	*	*	*	*	*	*
Under the Broom	97	*	*	*	*	*	*	*
Do This and Add Something	98				*	*	*	*
Concentration	98					*	*	*
Ghost	99					*	*	*
G. GAMES FOR OLDER CHILDREN								
Tracing Stars	100			*	*	*	*	*
Map-Making	101			*	*	*	*	*
Peanut Golf	102				*	*	*	*
Human Tic-Tac-Toe	103				*	*	*	*
Personal Bingo	104				*	*	*	*
Fortunes	105				*	*	*	*
Memory Teaser	106					*	*	*
Burglary	107					*	*	*
Quick Change	107					*	*	*
Identifying Months	108					*	*	*
Who Am I?	109					*	*	*
Hear It!	110					*	*	*
Smell It!	110					*	*	*
Feel It!	111					*	*	*
Novelty Competition	112				(Girls)	*	*	*
Post Card Identification	112					*	*	*

Games	Page	5 Yrs.	6 Yrs.	7 Yrs.	8 Yrs.	9 Yrs.	10 Yrs.	11 Yrs.
Categories	113					*	*	*
Typewriter	114						*	*
Spell It	116					*	*	*
Scrambled Animals	117						*	*
Advanced Fortunes	118						*	*
Cartoon Captions	119						*	*

H. ROTATIVE GAMES

Games	Page	5 Yrs.	6 Yrs.	7 Yrs.	8 Yrs.	9 Yrs.	10 Yrs.	11 Yrs.
Toothpick Balance	121					*	*	*
Bug	121					*	*	*
Horse Race	122					*	*	*
Bingo	123					*	*	*
Marble Roll-Away	123					*	*	*
Put and Take	123					*	*	*
Dots and Boxes	124					*	*	*
Bowling	124					*	*	*
Hangman	125					*	*	*

I. MISCELLANEOUS GAMES

Games	Page	5 Yrs.	6 Yrs.	7 Yrs.	8 Yrs.	9 Yrs.	10 Yrs.	11 Yrs.
Surprise Package	126	*	*	*	*	*	*	*
Magic Circles	128	*	*	*	*	*	*	*
Choosing Colors	129	*	*	*	*	*	*	*
Shoe Scramble	129	*	*	*	*	*	*	*
Chip Change	130		*	*	*	*	*	*
Crazy Auction	131			*	*	*	*	*
Memory Lotto	132			*	*	*	*	*
Bingo	133			*	*	*	*	*
Double It	133			*	*	*	*	*
Magic Boxes	134			*	*	*	*	*
Puzzle Boxes	136			*	*	*	*	*
Favors	136			*	*	*	*	*
Strings in Magic Boxes	136			*	*	*	*	*
Stunts in Magic Boxes	137			(Girls)	*	*	*	*
Five of a Kind	138			*	*	*	*	*
Snap Words	139				*	*		
Gold Digging	140					*	*	*

J. CREATIVE FUN

Games	Page	5 Yrs.	6 Yrs.	7 Yrs.	8 Yrs.	9 Yrs.	10 Yrs.	11 Yrs.
Barnyard Finger Puppets	145			*	*	*	*	*
Party Hats and Table Favors	146			*	*	*	*	*
Jolly Lollipops	148			*	*	*	*	*
Jingle Bells	149			*	*	*	*	*

How Shall We
Start the Games?

After you have had an opportunity to select the games for the party, it is important to consider a few general rules for playing these games.

The success of the game period depends in great part on you, the party-giver. You must be familiar with the rules of the games so that you in turn can explain them clearly to the children. This is especially important if the children are playing the game for the first time. Be willing to answer questions without showing impatience if the players don't understand just how the game is to proceed.

It is a good idea to prepare a list ahead of time, with each game listed in the order in which it is to be played. Under each one, check off the things which are needed to play the game. You will find handy check lists which can be used for this purpose accompanying each game. An example is given here.

WHAT'S NEEDED?

☐ Cardboard
☐ Scissors
☐ Tracing Paper
☐ Prize

FOR EACH PLAYER:

☐ Sheet of Paper
☐ Pencil

Assemble all of these supplies in a box or on a table near the game area. This will eliminate last-minute fumbling for the necessary items when the game is about to begin.

If prizes are needed, be sure that they are wrapped and on hand in a convenient spot. Decide beforehand if your child is to give out the prizes, or if each winner is to be allowed the fun of selecting his own. Set up a display of unwrapped prizes if you have decided to award prizes according to the number of stars earned during the game period (see "Shall We Have Prizes?" on page 23).

Cleaning up will be that much easier if you place a large carton near the game area. Wrapping papers from the prizes and discarded game materials can be deposited on the spot. This keeps the game area uncluttered and makes it easier to go on to the next game.

When you have everything on hand for playing the games, it is time to begin. The manner in which you invite the children to play is most important. Never ask, "Do you want to play this game?" You are apt to evoke a loud "No!" which will shake your confidence tremendously if you are doing this for the first time. Just assume that everyone is going to play the games that have been planned for them. A smiling invitation for the children to join you on the floor for the game you are about to play is far more effective when accompanied by your calm conviction that the children will do exactly that!

For some games it is necessary to select certain children to "go first." Often the party child feels that this is his privilege. However, it is quicker and hard feelings are less apt to result if you do the choosing, in an impartial manner. Since it is his birthday, attention is sure to be focused on your child anyway. Therefore, during the game period it is probably better for your child to remain as much a part of the group as possible by joining in with the other children as one of the players.

Occasionally you will encounter a child who refuses to enter into the games. Don't force this child to play, but leave room for him and accept him calmly if he decides to join the group. Some children watch from the sidelines through several parties before deciding to participate in the games.

There is the possibility that you may have to deal with a serious "troublemaker." If, despite your efforts to have him enjoy himself, a child persists in interfering with the fun of the group, it may become necessary for you to remove him from the room and explain firmly what behavior is expected of him if he wishes to remain at the party.

If several children express disinterest in a particular game, go on to the next one on your list. Perhaps you have chosen a game that is too easy, or too involved, or just not interesting to that particular group. If you have planned a swiftly paced party, with diversified games, you will be sure to interest every child before the game period is over.

Now that you have completed all of your preliminary planning, your preparations, and your program, it is time to begin your party. For a last-minute reminder, consult the Party-Giver's Check List on pages 150-151.

Games for the Youngest

On these 14 pages you will find a collection of games for very young children. These games involve little or no preparation and are easy to explain to the children. They take very little time to play—an asset since the youngest party-goers usually have short attention spans. Somewhat older children may enjoy these games too.

Animals Fly

Ages: 5-6   No. of Players: 6-15

WHAT'S NEEDED?

Nothing

PREPARATION
None.

PRESENTATION

1. Have the children stand or sit in a semicircle facing you. Explain that you are going to call out something like "Robins fly!" and that every child must flap his arms like wings. However, you may say "Elephants fly!" Then no one should wave his arms.

2. Practice a few times, using the names of animals that do or do not fly, until you think the children understand what to do.

3. Then announce that the game is starting. From that point on, any child who does not wave his arms when you mention an animal that can fly is out. Any child who waves his arms when you call out out an animal that cannot fly is also out.

4. Call out the animals' names as rapidly as possible. Continue playing until only one child is left. This child is the winner.

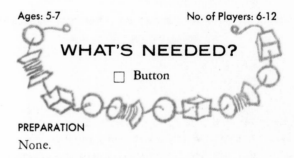

Beast, Bird, Fish

Ages: 5-7   No. of Players: 6-15

WHAT'S NEEDED?

☐ Beanbag or Large Ball

PREPARATION

None.

PRESENTATION

1. Ask the children to sit in a large circle. Sit in the center with the beanbag or ball.

2. Call out either "Beast," "Bird," or "Fish." At the same time toss the beanbag or ball to one player and begin counting "One, two, three, four, five."

3. This player must name correctly an animal from the category you have called out by the time you reach "five." Otherwise, he must change places with you and become "It."

If his answer is satisfactory, he tosses the beanbag or ball back to you, and the game continues. You cannot leave the center of the circle until someone responds incorrectly to your call of "Beast," "Bird," or "Fish." Continue playing in a lively manner for about ten minutes.

Button, Button

Ages: 5-7   No. of Players: 6-12

WHAT'S NEEDED?

☐ Button

PREPARATION

None.

PRESENTATION

1. Sit down with the children in a circle. Choose one child to be "It" and give him the button.

2. Turning his back on the group, the child places the button in one of his hands. He makes both hands into fists.

3. Holding both hands in front of him, he stands before one child in the circle. This child points to one hand.

4. "It" opens his hand. If that hand contains the button, the child guessing correctly becomes "It" and continues the game around the circle. If the button was in his other hand, "It" hides the button again, and goes on to the next player. If possible, try to continue playing the game until all of the children have had a chance to hide the button.

Games for the Youngest

Picture Lotto

Ages: 5-7   No. of Players: 6-12

WHAT'S NEEDED?

- [ ] Picture Lotto—2 Different Commercial Sets
      OR
- [ ] Colored Construction Paper
- [ ] Ruler
- [ ] Scissors
- [ ] 6 Different Pictures in Duplicate for Each Player
- [ ] Paste
- [ ] Large Envelope or Paper Bag

PREPARATION

If you do not have two different sets of Picture Lotto already on hand, you can make your own. For 12 players, cut 12 pieces of construction paper in pastel colors so that each measures 6 x 9 inches. Using a ruler, mark off six 3-inch-square boxes on each sheet.

Cut out six 3-inch squares for each child from the remaining sheets of construction paper. For 12 players you will need 72 of these squares.

Purchase two identical books (inexpensive picture dictionaries, or books on animals, plants, birds, or trucks are excellent choices) at a variety store. Cut out six different pictures in duplicate for each child. For 12 players you will need 72 different pictures in duplicate. Paste one of the pictures in a square on one of the large sheets. Paste the corresponding picture on one of the separate 3-inch squares.

Mix the small squares. Place them in a large envelope or paper bag.

PRESENTATION

1. Give each child one large sheet or card. Ask them to sit down in a circle with you.

2. Explain that you are going to draw one square at a time out of your bag. Whoever has the matching picture on his large card may claim the small square and place it over the corresponding picture. Whoever covers the entire card first wins the game.

Small children are usually more interested in covering the complete card than in just finding one winner. You can easily continue playing for the second-place winner, and right on through to the twelfth-place winner!

Dog and Bone

Ages: 5-7   **No. of Players: 6-15**

WHAT'S NEEDED?

☐ Real Bone, or a Small Object
   Such as a Peanut

PREPARATION

None.

PRESENTATION

1. Stand with the group in a circle. Select one child to be the Dog. Tell him to crouch in the center of the circle and hide his eyes with his arms.

2. Place the bone on the floor behind him. Point to another child in the circle. This child is to tiptoe up to the Dog and steal his bone. Tell this child to return to his place in the circle and put his hands behind his back, holding the bone so it cannot be seen. Instruct the other players to put their hands behind their backs and pretend that they have the bone.

3. Now tell the Dog that someone has taken his bone. He is to stand up, open his eyes, and make three guesses as to who has taken his bone. He may have heard the footsteps of the person stealing his bone. This will help him to guess correctly.

4. It doesn't really matter if the Dog doesn't guess correctly by the third guess. He can be asked to hide his eyes again. However, it is better to choose a new Dog for several reasons. The child may enjoy being the Dog and will not try to guess correctly. Or, especially in the case of a young child, failing to guess correctly after two turns may be upsetting.

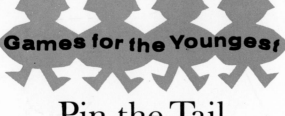

Games for the Youngest

Pin the Tail on the Donkey!

Ages: 5-9   **No. of Players: 6-12**

WHAT'S NEEDED?

☐ Pin the Tail on the Donkey—a Commercial Set with Separate Numbered Tails
     OR
☐ Old Pillow Slip
☐ Crayons
☐ Colored Construction Paper
☐ Scissors
☐ Cellophane Tape
☐ Blindfold (optional)

VARIATIONS Pin the Tail on the Donkey is certainly not a new game. It is included here more as a reminder, since it is practically a "must" for children in this age group. It is not necessary to have a commercial set. In fact, it might be more fun to try some of the variations suggested here.

Pin the Cow in the Bed: On an old pillow slip, draw a large four-poster bed with a colorful quilt and a pillow with an X in the middle. Using the pattern given below, cut the cows from construction paper. Use a different color for each cow, if possible. Or number the cows.

Pin the Dog in the Doghouse: Draw a large doghouse on the pillow slip. Mark an X in the doorway. Using the dog shown on page 39 as a pattern, cut the dogs from different colored construction paper.

Pin the Button on the Clown: Draw a large clown on the pillow slip, using the clown shown on page 41 as a guide. Draw in two of his three buttons. Mark an X where the third button should be. Cut the buttons from different colored construction paper.

(Continued on page 42)

Games for the Youngest

PIN THE TAIL ON THE DONKEY
(Continued)

Pin the Bell on the Christmas Tree: Draw a large tree with many decorations on the pillow slip. Put an X where the bell (or even star) should go. Using the pattern on page 40, cut the bells out of different colored construction paper.

Pin the Pipe on the Snowman: Draw a snowman (three circles, a hat, and a muffler) on the pillow slip. Place an X near his mouth. Cut the pipes out of different colored construction paper, using the pattern on page 40.

Pin the Flower in the Flower Pot: Draw a large red flower pot on an old pillow slip. Add several simple flower shapes, using the drawing on this page as a guide. Mark an X for the missing flower. Cut the flowers out of different colored construction paper.

PREPARATION

Choose which one of the variations your group will play. Prepare the drawing on the pillow slip. Cut the objects to be "pinned on" out of construction paper.

Tape the pillow slip to the wall so that the center of the drawing is at shoulder height for the players.

PRESENTATION

1. Set up a starting line about 6 feet away from the pillow slip. Distribute the objects to be "pinned" among the children.

2. Blindfold the child who is to go first. Turn him around three times and guide him toward the pillow slip.

Note: It is not necessary to blindfold the children. This is often frightening, especially for the younger child. Merely instruct the children to close their eyes and to keep them closed until you say to open them. There is remarkably little peeping, especially if you yourself sound convinced that everyone *will* keep his eyes closed!

3. Keep talking as the children approach the pillow slip. The first place on the picture that the child touches is where you must "pin" the object. Traditionally, we say "pin" the tail on the donkey, but actually cellophane tape is much easier and less dangerous for children to use.

4. Measure to see who came the closest to the area marked X. Don't encourage a booby prize.

Simple Simon

Ages: 5-9   No. of Players: 6-24

WHAT'S NEEDED?

Nothing

PREPARATION

None.

PRESENTATION

Like Pin the Tail on the Donkey, this game may well be familiar to you. However, it is included here because it is a favorite of children everywhere. Because of the action involved, it is a good "warming-up" activity to get the game period started.

1. Ask the group to stand facing you. Tell them that you are two people—Simple Simon and yourself. Explain that when Simple Simon tells them to do something, they must do it. However, if *you* tell them to do something, they must not do it.

2. Practice a few times with such commands as "Simple Simon says, 'Put your hands on your head.'" As you say this, perform the action yourself. Watch the group to be sure that they all do it.

3. Continue with such directions as "Simple Simon says, 'Clap your hands'" (you clap your hands), or "Simple Simon says, 'Touch your toes'" (touch your own toes).

4. When you see that the group is following you, try "Put your hands behind your back" (put your own hands behind your back). Pause to tell any child who does this that he should not have. Simple Simon didn't say to do it. Announce that from this point on, any player who does something that Simple Simon does not say to do is out. The players who do not follow commands preceded by "Simple Simon says" are also out. The last player to remain in the game is the winner.

Note: In groups that are familiar with this game, you may have difficulty eliminating players. Try rapidly alternating between "Simple Simon says, 'Put your hands on your shoulders'" and "Simple Simon says, 'Put your hands on your waist.'" Then when the group expects to do one

action right after the other, give the next direction without prefacing it with "Simple Simon says." Or give a command such as, "Move to the front of the room so that we can see you better." Many of the children will move forward, and thus be out.

I See Something

Ages: 5-9   No. of Players: 6-15

WHAT'S NEEDED?

Nothing

PREPARATION

None.

PRESENTATION

1. Sit with the group in a circle. Start the game by saying, "I see something red. Can you guess what it is?"

2. Go around the circle, allowing each child in turn a chance to guess the name of something he can see in the room which is red. The child who guesses correctly becomes the leader, and may choose an object of any color in the room. It's a good idea for him to whisper the selection to you, so that he won't forget it or change his mind as he goes along.

3. A few more difficult items to guess are your red lipstick, someone's white teeth, or the whites of someone's eyes. Continue playing, if possible, until each child has had a chance to be the leader.

Games for the Youngest

Fruit Basket

Ages: 5-8   No. of Players: 6-18

WHAT'S NEEDED?

☐ Colored Construction Paper
☐ Paste
☐ Scissors
☐ String

PREPARATION

The following fruits are suggested for this game: orange, apple, apricot, cherry, strawberry, lemon, grapefruit, peach, pear, pineapple, nectarine, lime, raspberry, banana, plum, watermelon, cantaloupe, grapes.

Choose a different fruit from this list for each player. Using the patterns given here, prepare a card for each child. Cut the fruits out of colored construction paper. Mount them on 9 x 12-inch sheets of construction paper. On each sheet tie a string large enough to go over the head of a child.

PRESENTATION

1. Have each child put on his fruit card. He will keep this fruit throughout the game.

2. Sit the children down in a circle, either on chairs or on the floor.

3. Select one child to go into the center of the circle. This child then calls the names of two fruits. The children bearing these names are to change places with each other. At the same time, the child in the center tries to reach one of their places first.

4. Whoever loses out on a place to sit must go to the center and call the names of two other fruits.

VARIATIONS   Use the names of only three fruits, and assign several children the same fruit. Seat them in order around the circle, such as orange, apple, pear; orange, apple, pear; orange, apple, pear. The child in the center calls the name of only one fruit. All children bearing that name change places with each other.

Instead of fruits, you can use animals, cars, flowers, or even colors.

Games for the Youngest

Three Up

Ages: 5-9   No. of Players: 8-18

WHAT'S NEEDED?

Nothing

PREPARATION
None.

PRESENTATION

1. Sit the group on the floor facing one wall of the room. Choose three children to stand with their backs to that wall, facing the rest of the group.

2. These three children will say, "Heads down!" At this command the seated children must put their heads down on their folded arms. Tell them they are not to look up again until they hear the command "Heads up!"

3. The three children in front of the group will then walk toward the seated children. Each will tap one child gently on the head and then return to his position against the wall.

Explain to the children that they must not look up when they are tapped. Instead they should raise one hand to show that they have been tapped.

4. When the three children have returned to their positions, they say "Heads up!" All the children may look up now. The three who were tapped stand up and try to guess who tapped them.

5. Call on these children one at a time. Say, "Andy, who do you think tapped you?" Andy may guess that Jimmy tapped him. If Jimmy did tap Andy, Andy goes to the wall and Jimmy sits down. If Jimmy says, "No, I did not tap Andy," then Jimmy remains at the wall and Andy sits down.

6. Continue playing until all the children who were tapped have had chances to guess. If no one guesses correctly, have the three children tell which persons they tapped. Then have the children who are now up say "Heads down!" and play again. Ten minutes is a good length of time for this game.

Clapping Game

Ages: 5-10   No. of Players: 6-24

WHAT'S NEEDED?

☐ Prizes (optional)

PREPARATION
None.

PRESENTATION

1. Sit with the children in a circle. Choose one child to hide his eyes, either against a wall in the room or outside the room.

2. Before he hides his eyes, pretend that you are the leader. Begin some motion, such as clapping your hands or tapping your head. Repeat this motion over and over again. Ask the children in the circle to do exactly what you do.

PREPARATION
None.

PRESENTATION

1. Sit in a circle with the children. Choose one child to hide his eyes, either in the room or outside the room.

2. Choose another child to hide the object somewhere in the room. Explain to the children that they must all remember where the object is hidden. But no one must tell. Without speaking, they will help the child who is looking for the object.

3. Send the child out to hide his eyes. Ask the other child to hide the object. When he has done so, call the first child to come and look for the object.

3. When you change to a different motion, have the children change too, as quickly as they can. Caution the children not to stare directly at you. Instead they should glance quickly at you from time to time.

4. Now send the child to hide his eyes. Choose a leader by pointing silently to someone in the circle. Have the leader begin and change motions at least once before the child is called back into the room.

5. Call the child then, and ask him to watch the group carefully. Tell him he has three chances to guess who the leader is. If he guesses within three chances, the child who was the leader goes to hide his eyes.

6. If he does not guess correctly, theoretically he should be sent out of the room again. However, with little children it is more important for everyone to have a chance. Guessing correctly does not seem to matter too much.

This game does not really require prizes. They may be given, however, if the child guesses correctly within his three chances.

Hot, Warm, Cold

Ages: 5-10   No. of Players: 6-15

WHAT'S NEEDED?

☐ One Peanut, Button, Piece of Chalk, or Other Small Object

☐ Stop Watch, or Watch with Second Hand

4. Lead the group in clapping their hands. They are to clap very softly when he is "cold," or far away from the object. They will clap louder as he gets "warmer" and approaches the object. They will clap very loudly when he is "hot," or right on top of the object.

5. Continue playing until all of the children have had a chance to either hide their eyes or the object. It is not necessary to give prizes for this game. Children enjoy being timed with a stop watch. They like to know exactly how long it took them to find the object.

Games for the Youngest

Touch the Spot

Ages: 6-9   No. of Players: 6-15

WHAT'S NEEDED?

☐ Slip of Paper for Each Player
☐ Small Object (peanut or button)
☐ Pencil
☐ Blindfold
☐ Cellophane Tape

PREPARATION

Write one number for each player on a separate slip of paper.

PRESENTATION

1. Clear the center of the room. Place the object (peanut or button) just about in the center of the room.

2. Establish a starting line. Give each child one of the numbered slips.

3. Blindfold the first child. Turn him around a few times. Tell him to walk to the spot where he thinks the object is. When he reaches the spot, he must touch his forehead to the floor on that spot.

4. Tape his numbered slip where he touches the floor. Continue playing until each child has had a turn. The child who comes the closest to the spot wins.

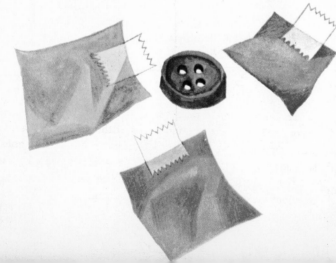

Telephone

Ages: 6-9   No. of Players: 6-15

WHAT'S NEEDED?

Nothing

PREPARATION

None.

PRESENTATION

1. Sit in a circle with the children.

2. Explain that you are going to whisper a sentence into the ear of the child on your right. That child then whispers what he hears into the ear of the child on *his* right. The results will be funniest if you start with an involved sentence. For example: "Harry's great-grandfather went fishing with a worm on a pin, and when he pulled the line up out of the water he found that he had caught a hatbox with a pink and gold hat in it that had two slits for someone's ears."

3. Continue the whispering around the circle until the last child receives the message. He repeats his message out loud.

4. Then announce what you really said. Usually there is quite a difference!

5. Now the child on your right makes up a sentence and starts it on its way around the circle. Continue playing until each child has had a chance to make up a sentence.

Time!

Ages: 7-9   **No. of Players: 6-14**

WHAT'S NEEDED?

Nothing

PREPARATION
None.

PRESENTATION

1. Sit in a circle with the children.

2. Choose two players to leave the room. They must decide on a certain hour of the day, such as six o'clock.

3. Then they return to the group and ask each child in turn, "What time is it?"

4. If the first child does not guess the time they have decided upon, they go on to the next child.

5. They continue around the circle until someone finally says, "Is it six o'clock?" Then the players doing the questioning both shout "Time!"

6. Whoever shouts "Time!" first asks the child who guessed correctly, "What do you want?" The child may tell him colors, animals, names, foods, or any other category he thinks of. He must also specify one, two, or three items in that category.

7. If, for instance, the child says, "Colors, two apiece," the first two players leave the room again. The one who called "Time!" first has first choice of two colors. The other player also chooses two colors.

8. They return to the room and ask the same child who guessed the time to choose either blue and gold or red and purple, for example.

9. The child makes his choice. The player whose colors were chosen remains this new child's partner. They leave the room to choose a new time. The other player rejoins the children in the circle.

The games which follow on these eight pages are guessing games. They are to be played by the middle age group of children (7- to 11-year olds). Since most of these games involve sitting in a circle on the floor, you can count on them for quiet periods.

Murder!

Ages: 7-11   No. of Players: 8-18

WHAT'S NEEDED?

☐ **Deck of Playing Cards**
☐ **Prizes (optional)**

PREPARATION

Select the two red kings and the ace of spades from the deck of cards. Then select enough number cards (use numbers 2 through 9) so that the total number of cards equals one for each player. Set aside the rest of the deck.

PRESENTATION

1. Have everyone sit in a circle. Tell them that two Detectives are needed to find the Murderer. Hold up the two red kings, and explain that these cards represent the Detectives. Then hold up the ace of spades. The person receiving this card is the Murderer.

2. Mix the cards and give one to each child. Ask each child to look at his card quickly and place it face down in front of him.

3. Ask the two Detectives to stand up. Collect the red kings from them, and ask them to leave the room. Collect the remaining cards.

4. Now ask the Murderer to stand up. He must quietly tap someone on the shoulder three times. Caution him not to speak out loud, or his voice may be recognized by the Detectives. The tapped Victim screams and falls over "dead" on the floor.

5. When the Murderer has returned to his place in the circle, call in the Detectives. Ask them to step into the middle of the circle. Together, they must go around the circle, asking each player in turn, "What were you doing at the time of the murder?"

Suggest several alibis, such as, "I was swimming in the goldfish bowl," or "I was eating electric light bulbs." The children will take it from there. The Murderer's alibi should always be false.

6. After all the witnesses have been questioned, give the Detectives one or two chances each to guess who the Murderer is. Facial expressions often give the players away.

Usually three or four rounds of Murder! are enough. Most children are content to play this game without prizes. However, the Detective who guesses the Murderer correctly may be awarded a small prize. Or the Murderer may receive one for "getting away with murder!"

Grandmother's Club

Ages: 7-11   No. of Players: 6-15

WHAT'S NEEDED?

Nothing

PREPARATION
None.

PRESENTATION

1. Sit in a circle with the children.

2. Explain the game as follows: "Grandmother has a club. Everyone wants to belong to this club, but no one can join unless he brings Grandmother a present. If she likes the present, you may join the club. If she doesn't, you must wait for your next turn to tell what present you would bring. There is a trick connected with what she would like to receive, but I can't tell you that until the end of the game. If you listen carefully, you may be able to figure it out."

(The trick is that each person must bring Grandmother a present which begins with the same letter as his or her own name.)

3. Begin the game by telling the children what you would bring. Don't hint that it has anything to do with your name. If your name is Harriet, try "hat" or "hamburger." Encourage one-word answers, such as "cake," rather than "a piece of cake."

4. Go around the circle counterclockwise, asking each child in turn what he would bring. If someone uses your answer, but has different initials, explain that it is correct for you but not for him.

Someone may guess correctly purely by accident. Capitalize on that guess by repeating: "*Richard* can bring a *radio*," "*Scott* can bring a *soda*," "*Nancy* can bring *nuts*," "What can *you* bring?"

5. If the game drags on with no correct guesses, try this: "Sue just guessed a lamp. She can't bring it, but there is someone else here who can. Let's go around the circle and have everyone say 'lamp.' No, Eddie can't bring a lamp. Gerry can't either. But, *Linda*, you may bring a *lamp*."

6. The trick will soon become clear to the majority of the children. Suggest that they explain it to those who still don't understand.

VARIATIONS   For Halloween, have them join the Witch's Club; at Christmas, Santa's Club; at Easter, Bunny Rabbit's Club.

Guessing Games

Party Clothes

Ages: 8-11   No. of Players: 6-18

WHAT'S NEEDED?

Nothing

PREPARATION
None.

PRESENTATION
1. Sit in a circle with the children.
2. Tell them to pretend that they are getting ready to come to this party. They must decide what to wear. Say the following sentence to them, without emphasizing any of the words: "In order to come to _____'s party, you must wear the right clothes."

3. Explain that you will go around the circle, asking each one in turn what he will wear. If he chooses the right clothes, he may come. If not, he will have to wait for his turn to come around again.

4. Start by telling what you would wear first, and then continue around the circle in a counter-clockwise direction. At first each player should name only one article of clothing. As the game progresses, it may be necessary to describe the entire outfit to make the answer more obvious.

(The trick is in the sentence about wearing the "right clothes." The children will assume you mean "correct" when you say "right." However, in this case you mean the clothes that the person on your *right side* is wearing.)

5. If no one guesses after a round or two, repeat the sentence, emphasizing the word "right." Caution the children who figure it out to look straight ahead while answering.

This game is hilarious when the guests are seated boy, girl, boy, girl. What boy will say "a pink dress"?

Odd or Even

Ages: 7-11   No. of Players: 6-24

WHAT'S NEEDED?

- ☐ 7 Uncooked Red Kidney Beans for Each Player
- ☐ Prize

PREPARATION
None.

PRESENTATION

1. Give each child seven beans. He is to hold them in one hand.

2. Take a few beans yourself. Slip one or two beans into your other hand.

3. Hold this hand out. Ask a child standing near you how many he thinks you have in your hand—one bean or two.

If he guesses correctly, explain that if the game were in progress, you would have to give him the beans. If he guesses incorrectly, show him that he was wrong, and you keep the beans.

4. Emphasize that they can have only one or two beans in the hand which they are holding out. Although the game is called Odd or Even, it is easier for the children to call out "one" or "two" when guessing the number of beans.

5. The children do not sit for this game. They may walk around the room and ask any other child, "One or two?"

If a child indicates to you that he has lost all his beans, whisper to him that he should just wait for someone to ask him now.

Some of the children may figure out that they cannot lose any beans if they refuse to ask the other children. If so, make a rule that anyone who answers must immediately ask the child who asked him.

6. After about five or ten minutes of play, warn the group that they have only one minute left to play. Then say, "Stop! Count your beans." The child who has the most beans is the winner.

Guessing Games

Truth or Consequences

Ages: 8-11   No. of Players: 10-20

WHAT'S NEEDED?

- [ ] List of True or False Questions (see page 55)
- [ ] 2 Baby Bottles
- [ ] 4 Balloons
- [ ] 2 Pieces of Bubble Gum
- [ ] 6 Crackers
- [ ] 2 Pieces of Rope, Each About 1 Yd. Long
- [ ] 2 Decks of Playing Cards
- [ ] 2 Paper Cups
- [ ] 2 Pencils
- [ ] Set of Anagrams
- [ ] 2 Magnets
- [ ] 2 Boxes of Paper Clips
- [ ] 2 Water Pistols
- [ ] Large Pan of Water
- [ ] 2 Candles
- [ ] Matches
- [ ] Prizes (optional)

PREPARATION

Write out a series of questions, either true or false, one for each of the players to answer. See the suggested list given on the next page.

Make the following preparations for the consequences. Fill each baby bottle with two ounces of water. Tie the same number of knots in each piece of rope, and plant the joker in the same spot in each deck of cards.

PRESENTATION

1. Explain that you are going to ask each player a question. Those answering incorrectly will have to compete in a consequence with another player who also answers incorrectly. Of course, everyone tries to answer incorrectly!

2. Tiny prizes may be given to the winners of the consequences.

CONSEQUENCES No. 1: The consequence for the first two incorrect answers is to see which player finishes drinking the water in the baby bottle first.

No. 2: Give each player a balloon. The winner is the one who blows it up, ties it, and breaks it by stepping on it first.

No. 3: Each player must chew up and swallow three dry crackers and try to whistle before his opponent does.

No. 4: Give each player a knotted rope. The winner is the one who unties all the knots first.

No. 5: Give each player one of the decks of cards. See who can find the joker first.

No. 6: Ask each player to pick out the letters spelling the party child's name from the box of Anagrams. See who can place them in order first.

No. 7: See which player can pick up the most paper clips with a magnet. Give each player three tries.

No. 8: Give each player a piece of bubble gum. See which player is able to blow the biggest bubble.

No. 9: Give each player a paper cup on the end of a pencil. See which one can twirl the cup for the longest time, without stopping the motion and without dropping the cup.

No. 10: Light the two candles. Float them on water or surround them by water. See which player can put out the flame with three shots from a water pistol.

QUESTIONS FOR "TRUTH OR CONSEQUENCES"

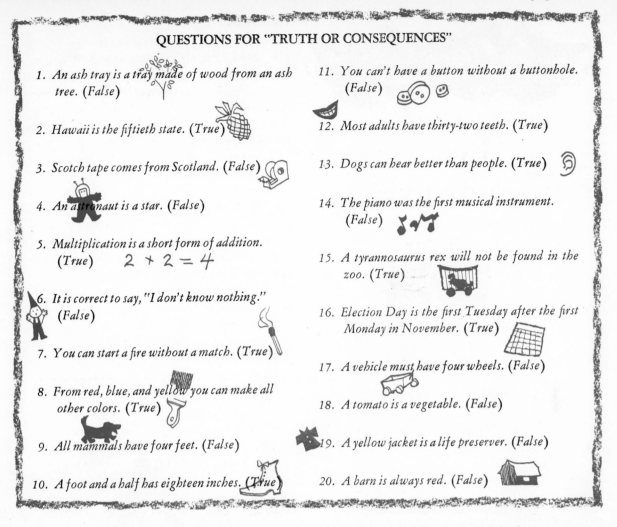

1. *An ash tray is a tray made of wood from an ash tree. (False)*

2. *Hawaii is the fiftieth state. (True)*

3. *Scotch tape comes from Scotland. (False)*

4. *An astronaut is a star. (False)*

5. *Multiplication is a short form of addition. (True)* 2 + 2 = 4

6. *It is correct to say, "I don't know nothing." (False)*

7. *You can start a fire without a match. (True)*

8. *From red, blue, and yellow you can make all other colors. (True)*

9. *All mammals have four feet. (False)*

10. *A foot and a half has eighteen inches. (True)*

11. *You can't have a button without a buttonhole. (False)*

12. *Most adults have thirty-two teeth. (True)*

13. *Dogs can hear better than people. (True)*

14. *The piano was the first musical instrument. (False)*

15. *A tyrannosaurus rex will not be found in the zoo. (True)*

16. *Election Day is the first Tuesday after the first Monday in November. (True)*

17. *A vehicle must have four wheels. (False)*

18. *A tomato is a vegetable. (False)*

19. *A yellow jacket is a life preserver. (False)*

20. *A barn is always red. (False)*

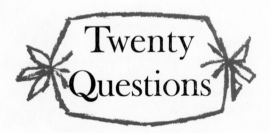

Twenty Questions

Ages: 8-11   No. of Players: 6-15

WHAT'S NEEDED?

Nothing

PREPARATION
None.

PRESENTATION
1. Sit in a circle with all the party children.

2. Send one child out of the room. After he has left, decide upon an object either within or outside the room.

3. Then ask the child to come back. He must find out what this object is by asking questions around the circle. The children may answer only "Yes" or "No," so he must word his questions accordingly.

4. Allow him exactly 20 questions. The question "Is it _____ ?" should be included in the 20.

5. When his 20 questions are used up, another child may leave the room and a different object can be decided upon.

VARIATION   Instead of an object, have the children choose a job or profession. Have the person who leaves the room guess "What's My Line?" in 20 questions.

Guessing Games

Beans Aplenty!

Ages: 8-11　　　**No. of Players: 6-32**

WHAT'S NEEDED?

☐ Glass Jar with Screw Top (empty peanut butter or mayonnaise jar)
☐ Uncooked Red Kidney Beans or Tiny Candies
☐ Cellophane Tape
☐ Paper and Pencil for Each Player
☐ Prize (optional)

PREPARATION

Count out a number of beans or candies—about 179 or 183—and place them in the jar. Write the exact number on a small piece of paper. Tape this paper to the underneath side of the jar top. Screw the top on the jar.

PRESENTATION

1. Show the jar to the children. Explain that the player who guesses closest to the correct number of beans or candies in the jar is the winner. This is a good game to play as the children are arriving at the party.

2. Let each child handle the jar, but point out that it is useless for them to try to count each bean or candy individually.

3. Ask each child to write his name and the number he's guessed on a separate slip of paper. Collect all the papers. Remove the jar top and compare the correct number with those on the slips. If you used beans, a prize should be given to the winner. If you used candies, the jar and its contents can serve as the prize.

Boots without Shoes

Ages: 9-11   No. of Players: 6-18

WHAT'S NEEDED?

Nothing

PREPARATION

None.

PRESENTATION

1. Sit in a circle with the children.

2. Tell them that you are going to ask them to say something. Also tell them that there is a trick to the game.

3. Say "Say boots without shoes" without emphasizing any of the words. Ask the child on your right to repeat what you told him to say. Go right around the circle.

4. If someone said the phrase correctly, indicate at the end who it was. (The trick is that you are telling the children to say *boots* without saying shoes. Thus the only correct response is just the single word "boots.")

5. If no one said the phrase correctly, go around the circle again. Most children will try to imitate an inflection in your voice. Or perhaps they will try to copy the position of your feet or hands.

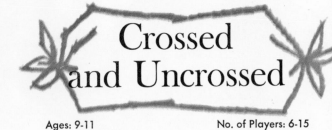

Crossed and Uncrossed

Ages: 9-11   No. of Players: 6-15

WHAT'S NEEDED?

☐ Scissors

PREPARATION

None.

PRESENTATION

1. Sit down in a circle with the children. For this game, it is better to sit on chairs.

2. Tell the children that there is a trick to this game and that they must watch you very closely. If they cannot guess the trick, promise to tell them what it is at the end of the game.

3. You are going to pass the scissors to the player on your right, and say aloud what you are doing.

(The trick lies not in how you pass the scissors —crossed or uncrossed—but in the position of your legs as you pass the scissors. Your feet are either *crossed* or *uncrossed*.)

4. If you start with your feet crossed, then you say to the next player, "I am passing the scissors crossed." If he is sitting with his feet straight, he should say, "I received the scissors uncrossed." If he stays that way, he should say, "And I am passing them uncrossed." However, if he changes the position of his feet, then he should say, "I received them uncrossed, and I am passing them crossed."

5. As leader, you will tell each player whether he is passing the scissors correctly. The children will undoubtedly try to vary the way the scissors are passed. They may open the blades and say they are "crossed," or close the blades and say they are "uncrossed." But the position of the blades is not important at all!

6. Continue playing for a few rounds. If the children are not catching on, cross or uncross your feet very obviously when it is your turn.

Games of Skill

These six pages all contain action games. The children will enjoy a few of these after sitting quietly through the guessing games. You will find that the "skills" that are required are not terribly demanding.

Feeding the Elephant

Ages: 5-9   No. of Players: 6-15

WHAT'S NEEDED?
☐ Colored Construction Paper (two 9" x 12" sheets, one gray, one pink)
☐ Paper Fasteners
☐ 5 Peanuts in Shells
☐ Paper and Pencil, for Scoring
☐ Prize

PREPARATION
Place the gray sheet of paper on top of the pink paper. Roll into a cylinder, with a 1-inch overlap. Fasten with paper fasteners.

PRESENTATION
1. Sit down in a circle with the children. Show them the paper roll and ask them to guess what it represents. If they have trouble guessing, show them the peanuts. Tell them, "We couldn't fit the whole elephant through the door, so we just brought his trunk."

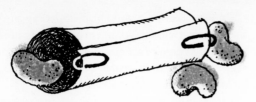

2. Place the "elephant's trunk" horizontally in the center of the circle. Face one open end toward the child who is to go first.

3. Give the child three peanuts. (Keep the other two in reserve in case of an emergency!) Explain that each player will be given a chance to "feed the elephant." The object is to toss the peanuts one at a time into the elephant's trunk. If the peanut goes completely through, you may announce that the elephant swallowed that one immediately!

Paper Toss

Ages: 5-9   **No. of Players: 6-15**

WHAT'S NEEDED?

☐ Three 8½" x 11" Sheets of Paper for Each Player
☐ Bottom Half of a Small Box, about 4" x 4" x 1"
☐ Paper Bag
☐ Prize

PREPARATION

Take each sheet of paper and crumple it into a ball. Place all the balls in a paper bag.

PRESENTATION

1. Sit in a circle with the children. Give each child three paper balls.

4. Write each child's name on your paper, in order around the circle. Enter each child's score as follows: one point for each peanut that enters the trunk.

5. Rotate the trunk slightly for each player. If too many children receive three points on the first round, make the circle larger for the second round. Usually three rounds are played. Announce the number of rounds you intend to play at the start of the game.

6. The winner is the child who has fed the most peanuts to the elephant at the close of the last round. Play off any ties. The children may enjoy hearing you add up the total number of peanuts the elephant has consumed!

If you have a whole bag of peanuts on hand, you may wish to reward each child with the number of peanuts he fed to the elephant.

2. Place the small box in the center of the circle. If a perfectly shaped circle is not possible in your room, you may need to move the box so that it is the same distance from each child as he takes his turn.

3. Do not allow the children to throw the balls at random. Explain that they must go around the circle, with each child tossing one ball as his turn comes up.

When a ball lands in the box, remove it and drop it into your bag. If a ball misses the box, return it to the child who threw it. If too many children seem to miss the box, you may wish to make the circle smaller at the end of the first round.

4. Continue tossing until one child has no paper balls left. He is the winner. Finish out that round, however, so that all the players have the same number of turns.

If, at the end of the round, you have several winners, give each one an extra ball. Have them play off the tie.

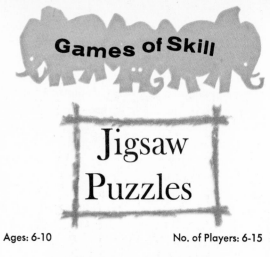

Games of Skill

Jigsaw Puzzles

Ages: 6-10   No. of Players: 6-15

WHAT'S NEEDED?

- ☐ Identical Picture Post Cards, 1 for Each Player
- ☐ Sandwich Bag or Plain Envelope for Each Player
- ☐ Pencil
- ☐ Carbon Paper
- ☐ Scissors
- ☐ Prize

PREPARATION

On the back of a picture post card, draw zigzag shapes as shown. For younger children, divide the card into five shapes. For older children, use nine shapes. Using carbon paper, transfer these shapes identically to the other post cards.

Label all five (or nine) pieces on one card with the letter A. Then cut out the pieces. Place them in a sandwich bag or envelope marked A. Label all the pieces on the second card B. Continue for this card and for all the remaining cards as you did for A.

PRESENTATION

1. Settle each child on the floor with a good space in front of him in which to work.

2. Distribute the envelopes containing the puzzle pieces among the children. Explain that the object of the game is to see who can put the puzzle together first.

3. When you say "Go!" the children are to open their envelopes and begin working on the puzzles. The first child finished is the winner.

The children may keep their puzzles. Or you may wish to save them to use another time.

Marble Roll-Away

Ages: 6-11   No. of Players: 6-15

WHAT'S NEEDED?

☐ Shoe Box
☐ 3 Marbles
☐ Scissors
☐ Crayon
☐ Paper and Pencil, for Scoring
☐ Prize

PREPARATION

Cut five square openings along one edge of the long side of the box, as shown. Make the center opening the smallest. With a crayon, mark it 10. Make the two end openings of medium size, and mark them 5. The other two holes should be fairly large, and marked 1.

PRESENTATION

1. Sit in a circle with the children. Write their names on your paper in counterclockwise order.

2. Place the box in the center of the circle, with the numbered openings facing the first player. Give this player the three marbles.

3. Explain that each player in turn is to roll the three marbles toward the box, one at a time. Ask the children sitting next to the player to call out the number if the marble goes through one of the openings.

4. Write the score of each player next to his name. Turn the box slightly to face each new player.

5. Decide in advance how many rounds of Marble Roll-Away you will play. Three is usually a good number. Add up the total scores of three rounds for each player. The winner is, of course, the child with the highest score.

Games of Skill

Stringing Straws

Ages: 5-11   No. of Players: 6-18

WHAT'S NEEDED?

☐ Shoelaces, 1 for Each Player
☐ Colored Construction Paper
☐ Scissors
☐ Box of Paper Drinking Straws

PREPARATION

Cut the paper drinking straws into pieces less than ½ inch in length. Cut 1-inch squares of colored construction paper, about 50 for each child. Poke a tiny hole in the center of each square. Tie a knot at one end of each shoelace.

PRESENTATION

1. Seat the children in a circle. Give each child one shoelace. Also place a small pile of cut straws and squares in front of each child.

2. Show the children how to alternate straws and squares by stringing a few on an extra shoelace.

3. Explain that when you say "Go!" each child is to begin stringing straws and squares on his shoelace. When you say "Stop!" each one must hold his lace high in the air.

4. Push the straws and squares down on each shoelace and see whose is the longest. You may decide not to say stop until one of the children claims to have finished the entire shoelace. Younger children may want to keep theirs to wear as necklaces.

Cotton Ball Toss

Ages: 6-10   No. of Players: 6-15

WHAT'S NEEDED?

☐ Large Piece of Oaktag
☐ Poster Paints or Crayons
☐ Absorbent Cotton
☐ Scissors
☐ Paper and Pencil, for Scoring
☐ String or Yarn
☐ Prize

PREPARATION

Draw a large head of a clown on a piece of oaktag. Use the drawing on the opposite page as a guide for coloring with poster paints or crayons. For his mouth, cut out a circle abut 5 inches in diameter.

Using absorbent cotton, form three balls about the size of tennis balls. Wrap them with string or yarn so they won't come apart.

PRESENTATION

1. Prop the clown against a chair or low table so that the cotton balls can be tossed through the mouth.

2. Establish a throwing line about 6 feet away.

3. Give the first child the three cotton balls. Explain that he should toss them one at a time.

4. As each child has his turn, write down how many balls enter the clown's mouth. Two rounds are usually sufficient for this game.

5. Total the scores. The child having the highest score is the winner.

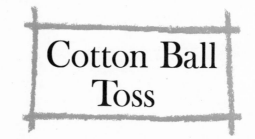

Hunts

All children love to hunt for things. It doesn't matter whether they are looking for candy kisses, pieces of string, or paper animals—the mad scramble is the same. On these 16 pages you will find all kinds of hunts, including scavenger hunts and treasure hunts, to keep your guests interested and busy party participants.

Candy Hunt

Ages: 5-11   No. of Players: 6-24

WHAT'S NEEDED?

- ☐ Wrapped Candies (sour balls, caramels, coins, miniature bars and rolls)
- ☐ Sandwich Bag for Each Player

PREPARATION

Before the guests arrive, hide the candies around the room. Write the children's names on the sandwich bags.

PRESENTATION

1. Give out the bags and tell the children to collect as many candies as they can. Each child may keep all that he finds.

2. Let the children select one or two candies to eat right away. Stow the bag with the remaining candies inside each child's "take-home" bag. (See page 22.)

Have a few extra candies on hand for any children who seem to be having difficulty finding their own.

String Hunt

Ages: 5-10   No. of Players: 6-15

WHAT'S NEEDED?

- ☐ Ball of String
- ☐ Scissors
- ☐ Prize

PREPARATION

Cut 60 to 80 pieces of string of varying lengths. Some should be as short as 2 inches, a few as long as 2 feet. Most should be 5 to 12 inches long.

On the day of the party, "hide" each piece of string in a separate place.

PRESENTATION

1. Ask the children to stand in the middle of the room. Point out to them some of the more obvious strings.

2. Explain that when you say "Go!" each child is to find and hold on to as many strings as he can. Tell the children that the strings are not all the same length, and that the winner will be the player whose strings form the longest line—not the player who collects the most strings!

3. After all or most of the strings have been found, ask the children to sit in a single line on one side of the room. Take the first child's strings and lay them end to end on the floor. Take the next child's strings and lay them end to end, parallel to the first child's. Continue doing this until all the strings have been laid out on the floor. The winner is the child with the longest line of strings.

Animal Hunt

Ages: 5-9 No. of Players: 6-24

WHAT'S NEEDED?

☐ Colored Construction Paper
☐ Tracing Paper
☐ Scissors
☐ Prize

PREPARATION

Using one of the patterns given here, trace and cut out about eight small animals for each child. Hide these about the room before the party.

PRESENTATION

Tell the children that, on your signal, they are to collect as many paper animals as they can. The child who finds the most is the winner.

VARIATIONS Use orange pumpkins for Halloween, trees for Christmas, bells for New Year's, hearts for Valentine's Day, hatchets for Washington's Birthday, and shamrocks for St. Patrick's Day.

Enlarge patterns by following the directions on page 8.

Hunts

Scavenger Hunts

When they hear the words "Scavenger Hunt," most people immediately think of wild forays into the night in search of all manner of spine-chilling treasures. On the following pages we have given you suggestions for one such typical outdoor scavenger hunt. In addition, we have also included several indoor variations. You will find these especially well suited to younger children. They are also a boon for families living in apartments or in sparsely populated neighborhoods.

A. LIMITED TO AN APARTMENT OR ONE HOUSE

Ages: 7-11   No. of Players: 6-16

WHAT'S NEEDED?

☐ List of Items for Each Player (see next page)
☐ Pencil and Paper Bag for Each Player
☐ 96 Items Listed on Next Page
☐ Prize

PREPARATION

The twelve lists on the next page each contain eight items. If you have twelve players, duplicate each list once. If you have six players, put lists I and II together on one piece of paper, III and IV together, and so on, so that each player will have to find 16 items. If you have 16 players, use the first six items on each list for players 1 through 12. Take items 7 and 8 from lists I, II, and III for player 13; from IV, V, and VI for player 14; from VII, VIII, and IX for player 15; from X, XI, and XII for player 16. If you have eight players, use lists I through VIII. If you wish, you may add 4 items to each of these lists from the remaining lists (IX through XII), giving each player 12 items to find.

Assemble all of the items needed for the hunt. Just before the party is to begin, place these items around the house or apartment. They should be in plain sight. Try not to put items from the same list next to each other.

PRESENTATION

1. Give each player a list, a paper bag, and a pencil to check off the items as he finds them.
2. Emphasize that all of the items can be found without opening any closets or bureau drawers. Be sure that each child can read every item on his list.
3. Tell the children that the first one to return to you with all the items on his list checked off is the winner.

(Continued on page 68)

I
1. a safety pin
2. a brown shoelace
3. a Band-Aid
4. a calendar
5. an empty match folder
6. a 1955 penny
7. an eyeglass case
8. a red pencil

V
1. a hammer
2. blue thread
3. a fork
4. a red lollipop
5. a 1957 penny
6. shoe polish
7. a candle
8. a small mirror

IX
1. one picture post card
2. waxed paper
3. one left shoe
4. a plastic cup
5. a 1951 penny
6. a snap fastener
7. an ace of diamonds
8. a bracelet

II
1. a paper clip
2. a plaid sock
3. a 1-cent stamp
4. a bobby pin
5. cellophane tape
6. a 1954 penny
7. a piece of string
8. a rubber band

VI
1. a piece of cotton
2. silver foil
3. an ace of hearts
4. a 1956 penny
5. a photograph of a baby
6. a flowered handkerchief
7. a toothbrush
8. a flashlight

X
1. a piece of gum
2. a 1950 penny
3. a cake of white soap
4. tissue paper
5. an orange lollipop
6. a green crayon
7. one left boot
8. a No. 2 pencil

III
1. a door key
2. a black belt
3. a 4-cent stamp
4. a small ball
5. a tape measure
6. a flashlight battery
7. an ace of spades
8. a 1953 penny

VII
1. an eraser
2. a teaspoon
3. a bell
4. pink soap
5. a pen
6. a 1959 penny
7. a shoehorn
8. a purple crayon

XI
1. an empty spool
2. a 1949 penny
3. one right boot
4. one 3-cent postal card
5. a necklace
6. a thimble
7. red thread
8. a green lollipop

IV
1. a roller skate key
2. a white button
3. an envelope
4. a comb
5. a crochet hook
6. a toothpick
7. a paper tissue
8. a 1952 penny

VIII
1. a screwdriver
2. a soup spoon
3. a plaid hair ribbon
4. a lemon drop (candy)
5. a stapler
6. a 1958 penny
7. an emery board
8. a pink crayon

XII
1. a powder puff
2. an ace of clubs
3. a paper napkin
4. a hairpin
5. one right shoe
6. an empty wallet
7. a 1948 penny
8. a yellow crayon

Hunts

SCAVENGER HUNTS (*Continued*)

B. LIMITED TO AN APARTMENT BUILDING OR THE HOUSES ON ONE BLOCK

Ages: 9-11   No. of Players: 6-18

WHAT'S NEEDED?

☐ Prize or Prizes

FOR EACH PLAYER:

☐ Pencil
☐ Large Paper Bag
☐ List of Items and Addresses
☐ 2 Envelopes

PREPARATION

A few days before the party, check with your neighbors to see which ones will be home during the time of the party. Make a list of those who would not mind being called on by the scavenger hunters, and duplicate it for each of the players.

Also make duplicate copies of the list at the top of the next column for each of the players.

You Must Find:

1. a diamond
2. a *printed* picture of a spoon
3. one red hair and its owner's autograph
4. a pink thimble
5. four silver hairpins
6. one diaper
7. one band from a cigar
8. one piece of chalk
9. a 1955 penny
10. one wrapped lemon sour ball

Note: The diamond may be a real one or a diamond from a deck of cards. But don't tell the children this.

PRESENTATION

1. Give each player one copy of each of the lists, a pencil to check off items as they are obtained, a paper bag, and two envelopes.

2. Tell the children that they may call on only the houses or apartments which are on their lists. Remind them that they are not to annoy other people or to destroy public property. You may wish to have them travel in pairs.

3. Set a time limit of about a half hour. The children are to return at that time with as many of the items as possible. Whoever has collected the most items is the winner!

Ages: 9-11   No. of Players: 6-18

WHAT'S NEEDED?

☐ Prize or Prizes

FOR EACH PLAYER:

☐ Pencil
☐ Large Paper Bag
☐ List of Items (see below)
☐ 4 Paper Cups
☐ 4 Tissues
☐ 4 Rubber Bands

You Must Find:
1. something alive that flies
2. a cup of wet sand
3. a salamander or a worm
4. a cup of pink water
5. five pine cones
6. three rocks, at least 2 inches in diameter
7. seven leaves that have fallen from trees
8. a piece of string
9. two empty soda pop bottles
10. two pieces of charcoal, at least 1 inch in diameter

PREPARATION

Make duplicate copies of the list on the right for each of the players.

PRESENTATION

1. Give each player a copy of the list and a pencil to check off items as they are found. Also give each one a large paper bag and four cups, four tissues, and four rubber bands.

2. Set a time limit of about a half hour. Ask the children to return at the end of that time with as many of the items as possible. You may wish to have the children travel in pairs. Remind them not to annoy other people or to destroy public property.

3. Whoever returns at the end of the half hour with the most items is the winner.

Hunts

Advertising Slogans Hunt

Ages: 9-11   No. of Players: 6-18

WHAT'S NEEDED?

☐ Old Magazines
☐ Scissors
☐ Pencil and Paper for Each Player
☐ Prize

PREPARATION

Cut out 30 advertisements from old magazines. Choose ads with "catch" phrases. If possible, they should feature 30 different products, or at least different manufacturers.

Label each ad with a number from 1 to 30. (These numbers are only for your use in preparing the hunt and should be disregarded by the children.)

Place the clipped advertisements, containing the "catch" phrase and the name of the product, around the room in order from 1 to 30. Make a check list for yourself containing the number of each ad, the catch phrase, and the product being advertised. Cut the name of the product from each ad before the game begins.

Prepare a paper for each player, with the player's name, the numbers 1 to 10 listed vertically, and the phrase describing one product on each line. Each child will be required to identify only 10 of the 30 products. To prevent bunching up at one advertisement, you may wish to use the chart on the next page to guide you in making up the individual lists.

	I VII XIII	II VIII XIV	III IX XV	IV X XVI	V XI XVII	VI XII XVIII
1	4	7	2	6	11	5
2	12	20	11	28	23	18
3	24	14	17	19	4	10
4	18	27	23	30	29	22
5	26	1	8	12	7	13
6	10	16	19	3	20	27
7	29	30	5	21	16	2
8	15	25	13	15	26	14
9	22	6	28	9	1	25
10	3	21	9	24	17	8

The Roman numerals represent the players; the numbers from 1 to 10 at the left refer to the numbers 1 to 10 on the players' papers. The numbers in the boxes correspond to the catch phrases from 1 to 30 on your check list.

PRESENTATION

1. Give each player a pencil and one of the previously prepared sheets of paper.

2. Tell the children that there are 30 ads around the room, but that only 10 of the ads apply to each of them.

3. They are to locate the advertising phrases listed on their sheets of paper. Then they must find out what product the ad is trying to sell. Each product name should be written in in the space next to the corresponding phrase.

4. The first child finished with the most correct answers is the winner.

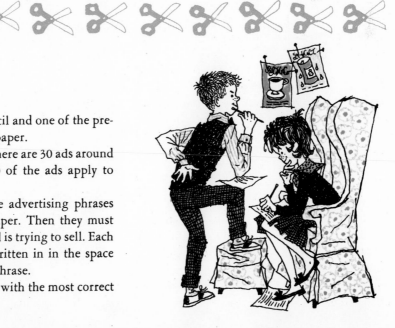

Hunts

Treasure Hunts

On these four pages we have given you two entirely different kinds of treasure hunts. The first one has the ideal spot for a buried treasure— the beach! The second one takes place completely indoors—perfect for the apartment dweller or a wintertime party.

Buried Treasure

Ages: 7-11   No. of Players: 6-14

WHAT'S NEEDED?

- ☐ Typing Paper
- ☐ Water Colors or Crayons
- ☐ Treasure (prize)

PREPARATION

Prepare a treasure map for each guest, using typing paper and water colors or crayons. The directions on your map should include natural landmarks of the beach where you are holding the party. For instance, "Go down the steps to the beach. Take ten paces toward the buoy. Take 18 paces toward the large rock. From the large rock, take 20 paces in whatever direction you think the treasure is buried."

Before the guests arrive, bury a treasure on the beach to correspond with the directions on the map. Your "treasure" might be a large bag of marshmallows to be toasted by everyone after the hunt.

PRESENTATION

Give each guest a map and turn them loose to seek the "treasure." To avoid accidents, be sure the children cover over any holes they dig.

Seashell Hunt

Before the refreshments are served or the water games begin, give each player a paper bag and see who can collect the most seashells within a given time limit.

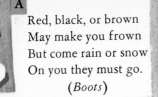

A
Red, black, or brown
May make you frown
But come rain or snow
On you they must go.
(*Boots*)

B
When night comes
And the sky grows dark
This will help you
To find your mark.
(*Lamp*)

C
The wicked one of *Snow White* fame
Always called this object by name.
(*Mirror*)

D
Even though you have no key
Find a clue where one should be.
(*Keyhole*)

E
'Tho far away, your friends are near.
Your voice they will be glad to hear.
(*Telephone*)

F
It would be hard to stand all day
So, big or little, these are here to stay.
(*Chair*)

G
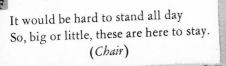
Between covers like these you will find
Every character who comes to mind.
(*Book*)

H

What time is it?
(*Treasure slip to be found under your wrist watch*)

Indoor Treasure Hunt

Ages: 9-11   **No. of Players: 7-14**

WHAT'S NEEDED?

☐ Four 3″ x 5″ Pads
☐ 9 Envelopes
☐ Treasure (prize)

PREPARATION

This game requires more advance preparation than most of the games in this book. However, you will find that careful preparation is the key to a very successful treasure hunt the day of the party.

Make one complete set of clues for each player. Write each clue on a separate sheet of paper from the 3 x 5-inch pads. Letter each clue sheet in the upper lefthand corner. Beneath each clue, in parentheses, you will find the name of the place or object to which this clue will lead the player. This is only for your information; do not copy these words on your clue papers.

If all the children were to reach the same clue at the same time, the game would become a mad scramble. Therefore, the chart on page 74 has been worked out to vary the order of clues. For this game, players will be referred to by Roman numerals.

Identify each complete set of clues (A to H) with a different Roman numeral (one for each player). Write the Roman numeral in the center at the top of each clue. Then arrange the clues under each Roman numeral in the order indicated on the chart. You will note that there is a number after each letter of the alphabet. Write this number in the upper righthand corner of the clue to which it corresponds on the chart.

(*Continued on page 74*)

Hunts

INDOOR TREASURE HUNT *(Continued)*

This chart has been worked out to help you vary the order of the clues for the Indoor Treasure Hunt.

I	II	III	IV	V	VI	VII	VIII	IX	X	XI	XII	XIII	XIV
A-1	B-1	C-1	D-1	E-1	F-1	G-1	A-1	B-1	C-1	D-1	E-1	F-1	G-1
B-2	G-2	F-2	E-2	D-2	A-2	C-2	B-2	G-2	F-2	E-2	D-2	A-2	C-2
C-3	A-3	G-3	B-3	F-3	E-3	D-3	C-3	A-3	G-3	B-3	F-3	E-3	D-3
D-4	E-4	A-4	G-4	C-4	B-4	F-4	D-4	E-4	A-4	G-4	C-4	B-4	F-4
E-5	C-5	D-5	F-5	A-5	G-5	B-5	E-5	C-5	D-5	F-5	A-5	G-5	B-5
F-6	D-6	B-6	A-6	G-6	C-6	E-6	F-6	D-6	B-6	A-6	G-6	C-6	E-6
G-7	F-7	E-7	C-7	B-7	D-7	A-7	G-7	F-7	E-7	C-7	B-7	D-7	A-7
H-8	H-8	H-8	H-8	H-8	H-8	H-8	H-8	H-8	H-8	H-8	H-8	H-8	H-8

Next, prepare nine envelopes and label them as follows:

No. 1: Not to be hidden; to be given to children at start of game

No. 2: To be hidden: inside or around BOOTS

No. 3: To be hidden: around LAMPS

No. 4: To be hidden: around MIRRORS

No. 5: To be hidden: around KEYHOLES

No. 6: To be hidden: around TELEPHONES

No. 7: To be hidden: around CHAIRS

No. 8: To be hidden: around BOOKS

No. 9: To be hidden: under your WRIST WATCH

Now place the slips of paper containing the clues in the proper packages:

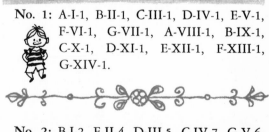

No. 1: A-I-1, B-II-1, C-III-1, D-IV-1, E-V-1, F-VI-1, G-VII-1, A-VIII-1, B-IX-1, C-X-1, D-XI-1, E-XII-1, F-XIII-1, G-XIV-1.

No. 2: B-I-2, E-II-4, D-III-5, C-IV-7, G-V-6, E-VI-3, H-VII-8, B-VIII-2, E-IX-4, D-X-5, C-XI-7, G-XII-6. E-XIII-3, H-XIV-8.

No. 3: C-I-3, G-II-2, E-III-7, G-IV-4, H-V-8, G-VI-5, E-VII-6, C-VIII-3, G-IX-2, E-X-7, G-XI-4, H-XII-8, G-XIII-5, E-XIV-6.

No. 4: D-I-4, D-II-6, F-III-2, H-IV-8, A-V-5, D-VI-7, D-VII-3, D-VIII-4, D-IX-6, F-X-2, H-XI-8, A-XII-5, D-XIII-7, D-XIV-3.

No. 5: E-I-5, F-II-7, B-III-6, E-IV-2, F-V-3, H-VI-8, F-VII-4, E-VIII-5, F-IX-7, B-X-6, E-XI-2, F-XII-3, H-XIII-8, F-XIV-4

No. 6: F-I-6, C-II-5, H-III-8, B-IV-3, D-V-2, B-VI-4, A-VII-7, F-VIII-6, C-IX-5, H-X-8, B-XI-3, D-XII-2, B-XIII-4, A-XIV-7

No. 7: G-I-7, H-II-8, G-III-3, A-IV-6, C-V-4, A-VI-2, B-VII-5, G-VIII-7, H-IX-8, G-X-3, A-XI-6, C-XII-4, A-XIII-2, B-XIV-5.

No. 8: H-I-8, A-II-3, A-III-4, F-IV-5, B-V-7, C-VI-6, C-VII-2, H-VIII-8, A-IX-3, A-X-4, F-XI-5, B-XII-7, C-XIII-6, C-XIV-2.

No. 9: Prepare one slip which says: "You have found the treasure!"

You are now finished until the morning of the party, when you will actually hide the clues. That morning, take one envelope at a time and hide each paper from it according to the directions on the outside. If it says LAMP, try to use more than one lamp to keep the clue areas from becoming congested. Fold each clue and hide it so that just the edge of the paper shows from the hiding place.

Save envelope No. 1 until you are ready to begin the game.

PRESENTATION

1. Give each player one clue from envelope No. 1. Explain that each child must find seven more clues before he comes to the treasure.

2. Point out that each player has a different Roman numeral on the top of his clue. During the hunt, each player may use *only* the clues bearing the same Roman numeral as his own. If he should find a clue with a different Roman numeral on it (and this happens often), he must quickly fold it up again and place it exactly where it was before. Stress that each child must be sure to do this, or the game will be ruined.

3. Have the children read their first clues. They are then ready to begin the search for Clue No. 2.

They may question you about the letters of the alphabet appearing in the upper lefthand corners of each clue. Tell them that these letters are not important and were just put there to help you in setting up the game. Their concern should be with the numbers from 1 to 8 in the upper right-hand corners.

4. As the various players find Clue No. 2, you may wish to check to be sure they have the right one. You may need to help some of the players to read the more difficult words in the clues. Be sure not to give away the hiding places in doing so!

5. Tell the children that they need not wait for the other children to catch up before going on to Clue No. 3. The first child to find the slip "You have found the treasure!" must be sure that he has all his clues in order. He then receives the treasure (prize).

Hunts

Paper Hunt

Ages: 6-11   No. of Players: 8-24

WHAT'S NEEDED?

- ☐ 3″ x 5″ Pads (1 blue, 1 yellow, 1 pink)
- ☐ Scissors
- ☐ Rubber Band
- ☐ Paper and Pencil, for Scoring
- ☐ Prize

PREPARATION

Separate the papers from each pad. Cut them in half so that each piece measures 3 x 2½ inches. Choose one blue, two pink, and three yellow pieces for each child. Pile them in order and fasten with a rubber band.

PRESENTATION

1. Give each child one set of previously prepared colored papers.

2. Divide the children into two groups. Explain that you are going to send one group into another room and keep one group with you.

Each child in each group must "hide" all six of his papers in his group's room. Each paper should be placed within reach, in a separate place. None should be hidden in closets or drawers!

3. After all the papers have been "hidden," the groups will change rooms to hunt for the papers. Since there are only a few blue papers, the blue will count 5 points each for the finder. The pink papers count 3 points each. The yellow papers count only 1 point each because there are many more of them.

4. Gather all the children in one room after the papers have been found. Assist them in adding up the points, and write down their scores. Of course, the child with the highest score is the winner!

Five Same Color Hunt

Ages: 6-9   No. of Players: 6-18

WHAT'S NEEDED?

- ☐ Colored Construction Paper
- ☐ Scissors
- ☐ Envelope
- ☐ Prize

PREPARATION

Cut 1″ x 5″ strips of construction paper—a different color for each player. Cut each strip into five equal squares. Mix the colors and place them in an envelope until the day of the party.

Just before the guests arrive, "hide" the squares around the room. Have at least a part of each square showing. Be sure not to put two squares of the same color next to each other.

PRESENTATION

1. Ask the children to stand in the center of the room. Point out some of the colored squares.

2. Explain that when you say "Go!" each child is to pick up one square. He must then try to find four other squares of exactly the same color.

If a child has difficulty in finding squares of a particular color, he may put down all the squares he is holding, choose another color, and start again. Be sure to emphasize that no one should pick up squares at random. Each player may hold only one color at a time.

3. The first child to hold five squares of the same color is the winner!

Anagram Hunt

Ages: 8-11   **No. of Players: 6-18**

WHAT'S NEEDED?

☐ Anagram Letters (1 or 2 sets, depending on number of players)
☐ Sandwich Bag for Each Player
☐ Pencil and Paper, for Scoring
☐ Prize

PREPARATION

Just before the party, scatter the anagram letters all around the room. Hide some rather well, but leave many in plain sight.

PRESENTATION

1. Give each player a sandwich bag and instructions to collect as many letters as he can.
2. Then have all the players sit on the floor. Allow enough room between players so that they do not get their anagram letters mixed up.
3. The object of the game is for each player to form words with the letters he has collected. No abbreviations, contractions, or proper nouns are allowed. The larger the word made, the higher the score.
4. Using the points given below, write the scores on your paper. The child with the greatest number of points is the winner.

SCORING

	No. of Points
Words containing 7 or more letters	10
6-letter words	8
5-letter words	6
4-letter words	4
3-letter words	2
2-letter words	1
Single-letter words	0
Misspelled words	0
Letters not used	*Subtract* 1

Hunts

B and C Hunt

Ages: 9-11   No. of Players: 6-24

WHAT'S NEEDED?

☐ Sheet of Paper and a Pencil for Each Player
☐ Prize or Prizes

PREPARATION

Fold each paper in half lengthwise. Label one column **B** and the other **C**.

PRESENTATION

1. Give each player a pencil and a previously prepared sheet of paper.

2. Explain that the object of this game is to see who can list the most objects in this house which begin wih the letters B and C.

3. Emphasize that all objects must be in plain sight. Limit the number of rooms which may be entered.

4. After 10 minutes warn the group that the time is almost up. Keep the children moving from one room to another so that all have an equal opportunity to observe. Give a second warning about a minute before you call "Stop!"

5. Ask each child to count his items (a total of 50 is not uncommon). Then ask who has more than 20, 25, 30, and on up.

6. Read aloud the paper having the most items. Ask the group to call out any duplications. The child with the greatest number of correct objects is the winner. (Correct spelling is not important!)

Instead of just one winner, you might also wish to give one prize to the child with the most objects beginning with B, and a second prize to the child with the most objects beginning with C.

B C B C B C B C B C

VARIATIONS For a Halloween party, ask the children to list the objects that are either black or orange. For a Christmas party, have them list the objects that are either red or green.

String Maze

Ages: 7-11   No. of Players: 6-15

WHAT'S NEEDED?

FOR EACH PLAYER:

- ☐ Different Colored Ball of String or Yarn
- ☐ Pencil
- ☐ Prize

PREPARATION

Tie a prize to the end of one ball of string or yarn. Hide the prize somewhere in the room—under a chair, a cushion, in a wastebasket. Unwind the ball of string completely, passing it around table legs, under furniture, and in and out of objects as you unwind.

Tie a pencil to the remaining end of the string. Repeat this procedure for each of the players. Don't worry about crisscrossing the strings; that only makes the game more fun!

PRESENTATION

1. Hand each child a pencil with the string attached. Explain that each string leads to a separate prize.

2. Ask the children to wind the strings on the pencils until they reach the prizes.

Card Hunt

Ages: 8-11   No. of Players: 6-18

WHAT'S NEEDED?

- ☐ 1 Deck of Playing Cards (no jokers) for Every 6 Players
- ☐ Prize

PREPARATION

Hide each card in a separate spot before the party begins. Do not use closets and drawers. Be sure that at least a corner of each card shows.

PRESENTATION

1. Tell the children that you have hidden the cards around the room. They are to find as many as they can when you say "Go!"

2. Allow them sufficient time to hunt. Then help them add up their individual points. The child with the highest score is the winner.

Number Cards 2-10 . . . . face value
Jacks . . . . 12 points
Queens . . . . 14 points
Kings . . . . 16 points
Aces . . . . 20 points

Elimination Races

The races described on these six pages are called elimination races. They are best played if the children are divided into groups of two, three, or four players.

After the first group races, the winner goes to a designated spot and the losers to another. The second group and third group then race. The race continues until all the children have had one turn. This ends the first round.

The winners of each group then race each other in the second round. Successive rounds are played until all but one player are eliminated. This child is the grand winner!

If you have an odd number of players, the last group in the first round may have three contestants rather than two.

Try to match the contestants for the first round according to height, weight, and age. Avoid, if possible, having brothers and sisters play against each other in the first round.

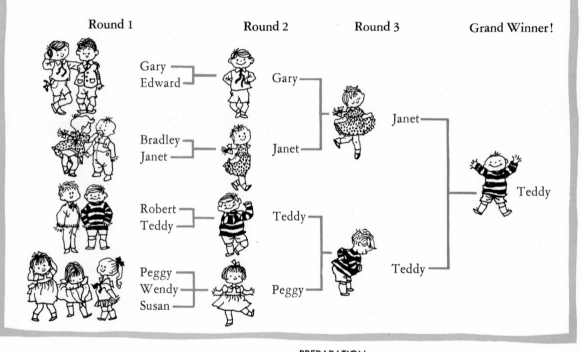

Round 1   Round 2   Round 3   Grand Winner!

Gary / Edward

Bradley / Janet

Robert / Teddy

Peggy / Wendy / Susan

Gary

Janet

Teddy

Peggy

Gary / Janet → Janet

Teddy / Teddy → Teddy

Janet / Teddy → Teddy

Push Peanut Race

Ages: 5-8   No. of Players: 8-24

WHAT'S NEEDED?

- ☐ 8 Peanuts
- ☐ 8 Pencils
- ☐ Prize

PREPARATION
None.

PRESENTATION

1. Designate a starting line and a finish line in the room. (Parallel sides of a living room rug work well.)

2. Line up the peanuts and pencils along the starting line.

3. Divide the children into groups of eight. Choose the first group for the first round. Explain that the peanuts are to be pushed, not hit, with the pencil across the room to the finish line.

4. Play as an elimination race until you have a grand winner.

Potato Race

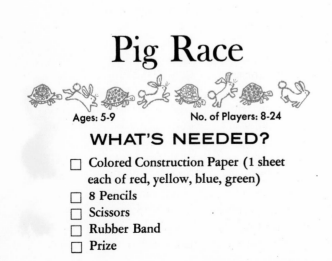

Ages: 5-11   No. of Players: 8-24

WHAT'S NEEDED?

- ☐ 4 Medium-sized Potatoes
- ☐ 4 Tablespoons
- ☐ Prize

PREPARATION
None.

PRESENTATION

1. Designate a starting line and a finish line in the room. Place the four potatoes along the starting line.

2. Divide the children into groups of four. Choose the first group for the first round. Give each one a tablespoon.

3. Explain that the players are to pick up the potatoes with the spoons without pushing against anything. They must carry them across the room to the finish line.

4. If a player drops the potato, he may pick it up again from wherever it has fallen. Play as an elimination race until you have a grand winner.

Pig Race

Ages: 5-9   No. of Players: 8-24

WHAT'S NEEDED?

- ☐ Colored Construction Paper (1 sheet each of red, yellow, blue, green)
- ☐ 8 Pencils
- ☐ Scissors
- ☐ Rubber Band
- ☐ Prize

PREPARATION

Using the pattern below, cut out one pig of each color. Also cut out nine 1-inch squares of each color. Mix the 36 squares and hold them together with a rubber band.

PRESENTATION

1. Mark off a race track in the center of the room. Use the pencils as markers, placing them parallel to each other, about 1 foot part.

2. Divide the children into groups of four. Choose the first group of players for the first round. Give each one a colored pig. Stand them shoulder to shoulder behind the starting line (first pencil).

3. Stand facing the "little pigs." Shuffle the colored squares in your hands. Without looking, draw out a square. Hold it up as you call out its color. If you have drawn red, the "red pig" steps over the first pencil and stands in the first space.

4. Continue drawing the squares. The first "little pig" to step over the last pencil is the winner. He goes to sit on the winner's side of the room.

5. Continue playing as an elimination race. The last "little pig" to remain in the game is the grand winner!

Rope Race

Ages: 5-11   No. of Players: 8-24

WHAT'S NEEDED?

- [ ] Ball of Thick Rope or a Clothesline
- [ ] Scissors
- [ ] Prize

PREPARATION

Cut two pieces of rope, each about 45 inches long. Knot each into a circle.

PRESENTATION

1. Seat the children in a line on one side of the room. Stand before them with one circle of rope in your hand. Demonstrate what each child will do when it is his turn: Extend your arms over your head, keeping your elbows straight. Pass the rope circle over your head and bring it down around your body. Step out of it and hold it high.

2. Choose the first two children for the first round. Give each child one of the rope circles. They are to stand with their arms out straight until you say the word "Go!" Then they begin to work the ropes down over their heads.

3. Continue playing as an elimination race (page 80) until you have a grand winner.

Horse Race

Ages: 6-11   No. of Players: 8-24

WHAT'S NEEDED?

- [ ] Cardboard
- [ ] Scissors
- [ ] Tracing Paper
- [ ] Red and Black Crayons
- [ ] Deck of Playing Cards
- [ ] 8 Pencils
- [ ] Prize

PREPARATION

Using the pattern on the next page, trace and cut four horses out of cardboard. In place of a saddle, draw a red heart on one, a red diamond on another, a black spade on another, and a black club on the fourth. Shuffle the deck of cards thoroughly.

PRESENTATION

1. Set up a course for the race by placing the eight pencils parallel to each other across the room, about 1 foot apart.

2. Choose four players for the first group in the first round. Give each player one of the previously prepared horses.

3. Ask these four "horses" to line up, shoulder to shoulder, behind the first pencil.

4. Stand near the finish line (last pencil), facing the "horses," with the deck of cards in your hands.

5. Turn over the top card and call out the suit. The corresponding "horse" takes one step forward, over the first pencil and into the next space. Continue turning over the cards and calling out the suits, as the "horses" advance. The first "horse" to cross the finish line wins this race. He goes to sit on the winner's side of the room, and will compete later with the other winners.

6. Shuffle the cards and continue playing with the remaining groups in the first round. Play as an elimination race (page 80) until you have a grand winner.

Stars and Straws Race

Ages: 6-11   **No. of Players: 8-24**

WHAT'S NEEDED?

- ☐ Paper Drinking Straws
- ☐ Scissors
- ☐ Colored Construction Paper
- ☐ Tracing Paper
- ☐ Prize

PREPARATION

Cut enough drinking straws in half so that you will have a half straw for each player. Using the star pattern on page 100, trace and cut out of construction paper one star for each member of one group. (See paragraph 4.)

PRESENTATION

1. Ask the children to sit in a single line on one side of the room. Establish a finish line with a chair, low table, or book placed at one end of the room.

2. Place two paper stars on the floor, about 2 feet apart, at the end of the room opposite the finish line.

3. Explain that the object of this race is to move the star from the starting line to the finish line without touching it with your hands. Demonstrate how this can be done with the straw: Place one end of the straw in your mouth. Bend down and pick up the star by inhaling through the straw. Hold your breath, walk across the room and deposit the star at the finish line.

4. It is advisable to play this race in groups of two. However, if you have a large number of players and your room is wide, you may wish to divide the players into groups of three or four.

5. Choose the first two (or three or four) players. Give them their straws. Be sure, especially with young children, that they know how to blow through straws.

6. Explain that they may touch the straws but never the stars. If a star drops, the player need not return to the starting line. He may start again wherever he is.

7. After everyone has played the first round, have the winners play each other, as in an elimination race (page 80). Continue playing until you have a grand winner.

Elimination Races

Tightrope Walking Race

Ages: 8-11   No. of Players: 8-24

WHAT'S NEEDED?

- [ ] 4 Equal Lengths of Cord, about 20 Ft. Each
- [ ] Prize

PREPARATION

Stretch the cords across the room, parallel to each other and at least 3 feet apart. Anchor both ends of each cord by tying to furniture legs or around books.

PRESENTATION

1. Show the children how to walk the "tightrope." Begin by placing the heel of one foot on the starting line. Proceed across the rope by placing the heel of the other foot directly against the toes of the first foot, until you reach the finish line.

2. Divide the players into groups of four. The winner of each group is the one who can walk the tightrope the fastest. Play as an elimination race (page 80).

Egg Race

Ages: 7-11   No. of Players: 8-24

WHAT'S NEEDED?

- [ ] Cardboard
- [ ] 4 Eggs
- [ ] Needle
- [ ] Bowl
- [ ] Poster Paints (optional)
- [ ] Prize

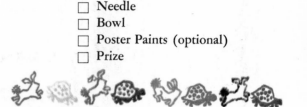

PREPARATION

Prepare the eggshells several days before the party. Make a small hole with a needle at both ends of each egg. Blow through one hole and catch the contents of the eggshell in a bowl. Dry the eggshells overnight.

For a special touch, decorate the eggshells with peasant designs, or faces, as shown here.

PRESENTATION

1. Establish a starting line on one side of the room and a finish line on the other.

2. Divide the players into groups of four. Place the eggshells along the starting line. Give each player in the first group a piece of cardboard.

3. Explain that the players are to fan the eggshells across the room and over the finish line. This is easier said than done, since eggs are not round!

4. Play as an elimination race (page 80).

Scoop Bean Race

Ages: 8-11   No. of Players: 8-16

WHAT'S NEEDED?

- ☐ 1 lb. Red Kidney Beans, Uncooked
- ☐ 2 Small Containers for Each Player
- ☐ Teaspoon for Each Player
- ☐ Prize

PREPARATION

Count out 30 to 50 beans for each player and place them in individual containers (plastic refrigerator boxes are ideal).

PRESENTATION

1. Establish a starting line and a finish line in the room.

2. Divide the players into groups of three or four.

3. For each player in the first group, place one container with beans in it on the starting line and an empty container on the finish line. Give each player a teaspoon.

4. Explain that when you say "Go!" they are to scoop up as many beans as possible with the teaspoon and carry them across the room to their container on the finish line. Allow exactly one minute for each group. The number of individual trips made does not count—just the total number of beans dropped in each empty container.

The children may have difficulty keeping their containers straight. Simply designate each pair of containers with different colored markers.

5. Play as an elimination race (page 80).

Newspaper Race

Ages: 8-11   No. of Players: 8-24

WHAT'S NEEDED?

- ☐ Sheet of Newspaper for Each Player
- ☐ Prize

PREPARATION

Tear each sheet of newspaper in half, so that you have two pieces approximately 12 x 14 inches for each player.

PRESENTATION

1. Establish a starting line and a finish line as far apart as the room will permit. If played outdoors, about 30 feet.

2. Using two pieces of newspaper, show the children how to walk across this designated area: Place one paper on the starting line and step on it with both feet. Place the second paper on the floor, as far in front of you as you can step with both feet, without stepping on the floor. Take a giant step!

Reach behind you and pick up the paper you just left. Place that paper ahead of you, step on it, and reach for the paper behind you. Continue to the finish line.

3. Choose four players for the first group in the first round. Continue playing as an elimination race (page 80).

Relay Races

On these eight pages you will find suggestions for 21 relay races—enough to make for a very busy, lively party. Relay races are best played out-of-doors or in a gym. However, they can also be run off in a fairly large room—preferably a recreation room or a family room.

Relay races are played in teams. These teams should be equal in number, with from four to eight players on a team. When there are more than 16 players, form more than two teams. If you have an uneven number of children, one team may be short a player. The first child on that team will always have to go first and last, so that the same number of players participates in each race.

The members of each team will stand or sit one behind the other. The first player on each team stands just behind the starting line. The teams stand parallel to each other, about 3 feet apart.

You may wish to prepare colored tags for the players to wear throughout the relay races. All members of one team will wear the same color. Besides being fun, it helps the players to identify their teams.

In a relay race, only the first person on each team starts at the signal "Go!" He does whatever is required for that particular relay, and returns to his team. He tags the right hand of the second person on his team and then goes to the end of his line. When everyone on that team has had a turn, he becomes first again. He raises his hand to signal that his team is finished—and has won!

Try to balance your teams in regard to age, height, weight, and dexterity before you begin the games. Whenever possible, keep brothers and sisters on the same team.

When you have more than two teams, score for first, second, and third places. Prizes are optional —the prestige of winning the relay, particularly an involved one, is often reward enough for the team members.

These relays are planned for from 8 to 32 children between the ages of 7 and 11.

Running Relay

WHAT'S NEEDED?

FOR EACH TEAM:
☐ Large Object, Such as a Chair

Place a chair some distance in front of each team. The players are to run around the chair and return to tag the next player. *Never* use the wall as a turning point!

Hopping Relay

Use the same chairs as for Running Relay. Players hop to and around the chairs. They return to their teams, hopping.

Jumping Relay

Use the same chairs as for Running Relay. Players place both feet together and jump to and around the chairs. They return to their teams, jumping.

Skipping Relay

Use the same chairs as for Running Relay. Players skip to and around the chairs. They return to their teams, skipping.

Combination Relay

Use the same chairs as for Running Relay. As the name suggests, the players go up and return with a combination of steps. Perhaps they might hop up and run back. Or they might run up and jump back. After playing a number of the relays described here, the children might enjoy suggesting their own combinations.

Overhead Ball Pass Relay

WHAT'S NEEDED?

FOR EACH TEAM:

☐ Large Ball, Such as a Basketball

The first player on each team holds the ball over his head. When you say "Go!" he passes it back over his head to the player behind him, who passes it back over his head.

When the ball reaches the last player, that player runs with the ball to the front of his team. He starts the ball back over the heads again. The game continues until the first player is at the head of the line again.

Under Leg Ball Pass Relay

Use the same ball as in Overhead Ball Pass Relay. The first player on each team holds the ball between his legs. When you say "Go!" he passes the ball under his legs to the player behind him. He in turn passes it under his legs to the player behind him.

When the ball reaches the last player, he runs up to the front of his team with the ball. He begins passing the ball down the line between the players' legs. The game continues until the first player is at the head of the line again.

Kangaroo Relay

Use the same ball as in Overhead Ball Pass Relay, and the same chairs as for Running Relay. The first player on each team places a ball between his knees. He jumps with the ball in this position to and around the chairs. He jumps back to tag the next player. The players may touch the ball with their hands only to pass it to the next player, or to pick up a dropped ball. A player cannot move while he has his hands on the ball.

Crawling Relay

The first player turns and faces his team. At the word "Go!" he crawls under the legs of all of his teammates. When he reaches the end of the line, he runs to the front and tags the next player. Then he returns to the end of the line so that the player just tagged can also crawl under his legs. The game continues until the first player is at the head of the line again.

Beanbag Exchange Relay

WHAT'S NEEDED?

- [ ] Beanbag for Each Team
- [ ] Colored Construction Paper
- [ ] and Scissors
  OR
- [ ] Chalk

Using construction paper, cut out two small circles for each team. (If circumstances allow, it is easier to draw the circles in chalk right on the floor.) Place one circle about 5 feet in front of the team, the other about 10 feet. Place a beanbag in the circle closest to each team.

At the word "Go!" the first player runs to the first circle, picks up the beanbag and deposits it in the farther circle. He then runs back and tags the next player. That player runs to the far circle, picks up the beanbag, and replaces it in the near circle. Continue alternating the beanbag until the first player is at the head of the line again.

Make a rule that the beanbag must be placed entirely within the circle—not just on the edge.

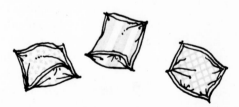

Bowling Relay

WHAT'S NEEDED?

FOR EACH TEAM:

- ☐ 3 Oblong Wooden Blocks
- ☐ Small Ball
- ☐ Paper and Pencil, for Scoring

Set up the blocks in a triangle, about 10 feet in front of each team. Give the first player on each team a small ball. Each player has one chance to "bowl." If he knocks over all three blocks, he scores 10 points for his team. One block is worth 3 points; two blocks, 7 points. Each player must chase the ball and replace the blocks before giving the ball to the next player. Speed does not count in this relay, only points.

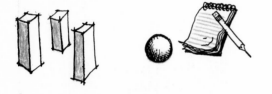

Treasure Hunt Relay

WHAT'S NEEDED?

- ☐ Wrapped Candies
  - OR
- ☐ Colored Construction Paper
- ☐ and Scissors
  - OR
- ☐ Inexpensive Prizes

Before the relays begin, hide the wrapped candies, animals made from construction paper (see page 65), or wrapped prizes around the room. Be sure to have at least one for each player. The first player on each team must find one object, return to his team, and tag the next player. This player must also find one object before returning to tag the next player in line, and so on.

Suitcase Relay

WHAT'S NEEDED?

FOR EACH TEAM:

- ☐ Small Suitcase Filled with:
  - ☐ Large Pair of Bluejeans
  - ☐ Large Pullover Sweater
  - ☐ Large Pair of Boots

Give the first player on each team a suitcase. At the word "Go!" each player must open the suitcase and put on the contents over his own clothing. He takes the suitcase and travels to a designated spot (a foyer or the other side of the room). Here he removes the clothing and repacks the suitcase. He returns and gives the suitcase to the next player on the team, who repeats the process.

Relay Races

Ball Balancing Relay

WHAT'S NEEDED?

FOR EACH TEAM:

☐ Empty Soda Bottle
☐ Jack Ball

Set the empty bottle at the turning point for each team. Give the first player on each team a ball. At the word "Go!" each player is to run to the bottle and balance the ball on top of it. He then returns to tag the second player, who runs up and brings the ball back to the third player. This player then balances the ball on the bottle again. Continue alternating in this way until the first player is at the head of the line again.

Ball and Spoon Relay

WHAT'S NEEDED?

FOR EACH TEAM:

☐ Teaspoon
☐ Jack Ball
☐ Chair

Give the first player on each team a ball and spoon. Each player must run to and around the chair, carrying the ball on the spoon. If the ball rolls off the spoon, the player must retrieve it, and continue running. The game continues until the first player is first in line again.

Water Carrying Relay

WHAT'S NEEDED?

FOR EACH TEAM:

☐ Large Paper Cup Filled
   with Water
☐ Chair

This game should really be limited to the outdoors! Give the first player on each team one of the paper cups. He may run or walk around the chair and back to the second player. When the first player is back at the head of the line, see which team has the most water left in its cup.

Snipping Strips Relay

WHAT'S NEEDED?

FOR EACH TEAM:
- [ ] 2" Strips of Paper, 3' Long
- [ ] Scissors
- [ ] Adult to Supervise

Ask the adults to stand at the turning points, with the scissors and long paper strips. The first player in each team must run up and cut a strip of paper in half lengthwise. The next player cuts a new strip in half. Continue cutting strips of paper in half lengthwise until the first player reaches the head of the line again. The adults can keep track of discarding the unused halves of paper after each player's turn.

Rope Relay

WHAT'S NEEDED?

FOR EACH TEAM:
- [ ] 45" Circle of Rope

Place the rope circles at the turning point for each team. The players run up to the circles and put them on over their heads. They step out of the circles and return to tag the next players, who run up and repeat the process. Continue playing until the first player is at the head of the line again.

Under the Broom Relay

WHAT'S NEEDED?

FOR EACH TEAM:
- [ ] Broom
- [ ] 2 Chairs

At the turning point for each team, place a broom across two chairs. The players, in turn, must run up to the turning point and slither under the broom before returning to tag the next player. Continue the game until the first player is at the head of the line again.

Relay Races

Thread the Needle Relay

WHAT'S NEEDED?

FOR EACH TEAM:
- ☐ Needles with Large Eyes
- ☐ Lengths of Wool
- ☐ Adult to Supervise

Ask the adults to stand at the turning points, with the needles and wool. Each player, in turn, must run up and thread a needle. Continue the game until the first player is at the head of the line again.

"Gone Fishing" Relay

WHAT'S NEEDED?

- ☐ Colored Construction Paper
- ☐ Tracing Paper
- ☐ Scissors
- ☐ Paper Clips

FOR EACH TEAM:
- ☐ Magnet
- ☐ Pencil
- ☐ String

Using the patterns shown here, trace and cut out at least one fish for each player. Place a paper clip in the mouth of each fish. Make a fishing rod for each team, consisting of a pencil, string, and a magnet.

Place a pile of fish on the floor in front of each team. Establish a "shore line" for the players to stand behind. Each player, in turn, must try to catch one fish before returning to tag the next member of his team.

For surprise bonus points, mark the fish with different point values on their undersides.

Elimination Contests

Among the games on these six pages you will recognize an old friend—Musical Chairs. All of the games in this group are called Elimination Contests. In each case the game is played until all but one—the winner—are eliminated.

Wonder Ball

Ages: 5-11   No. of Players: 6-18

WHAT'S NEEDED?

☐ Ball of Any Size
☐ Prize

PREPARATION
None.

PRESENTATION

1. Sit in a circle with the children. Pass the ball counterclockwise. Each child must pass, not throw, the ball. If it rolls away, the last child to have touched it must retrieve it and pass it on.

2. Tell the children that it's silly to pass the ball around and around for no reason. Instead have them chant: "Round and round the wonder ball goes, and where it stops nobody knows." Whoever has the ball on the word "knows" is out.

3. Play a few times just for practice. Then begin playing "for keeps."

4. When a child is out, ask him to move back out of the circle slightly, but have him continue chanting with the other children. Continue playing until there is only one child left—the winner!

5. If there are fewer than 10 players, you may wish to play for points. Then no one is out until he has two or three points against him.

Yes, No, Black, Blue

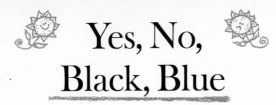

Ages: 5-9   No. of Players: 6-15

WHAT'S NEEDED?

☐ Prize

PREPARATION
None.

PRESENTATION

1. Sit with the children in a circle. Explain that you are going to ask them questions in turn. They must answer promptly. However, they must not use the words "yes," "no," "black," or "blue" in their answers, or they will be out.

2. Proceed around the circle, asking such questions as: "Are you eight years old?" "Do you like boys?" "What color is a blackboard?" and "Do you like ice cream?" The children will soon discover that "Maybe" is a good answer. You may have to eliminate that word also.

3. After the first round, announce that you will count up to five after each question. If the child does not answer by the time you say "five," he will be out. For the third round, reduce the count to three.

4. Play quickly, for the children who are eliminated soon grow restless. The winner is the child who most successfully avoids the use of the forbidden words.

One Out

Ages: 5-11   No. of Players: 6-18

WHAT'S NEEDED?
☐ One Penny for Each Player
☐ Prize

PREPARATION
None.

PRESENTATION

1. Ask the children to stand and join hands in a circle in the center of the room.

2. Walk around the room and place one penny for each player in a different spot. The children may watch where you put them.

3. Tell the players that you are going to say, "Get ready, get set, go!" On the word "Go!" they are to drop hands, pick up one penny apiece, and sit in the center of the floor.

4. The first time there will be a penny for each player. Ask the children to return the pennies to you and stand with their hands joined again.

5. Place the pennies around the room again. This time have one or two fewer pennies than children in the game. Whoever does not find a penny is out.

6. Use care in selecting "hiding places" to avoid bumped heads. When you are down to the last two players, do not let them see the hiding places you select. Occasionally place a penny on top of the head of a child who was eliminated fairly early in the game. This maintains interest for those on the sidelines. The last player to remain in the game is the winner.

Elimination Contests

Musical Chairs

Ages: 5-11   No. of Players: 8-24

WHAT'S NEEDED?

☐ Chair for Each Player
☐ Piano
    OR
☐ Record Player and Records
☐ Prize

PREPARATION

Arrange the chairs in the center of the room in a line or semicircle, with the chairs just barely touching. Face every other chair in the opposite direction.

PRESENTATION

1. Ask each of the children to sit on a chair. Then have them stand and turn to form a line for marching.

2. Tell them to put their hands on their heads. When the music begins, they are to start marching. They must not get out of line while marching.

3. When the music stops, each child must sit in a chair—even if it means getting out of line. If the only empty chair is facing in the opposite direction, the child must run all the way around the chairs to reach it. No short cuts between chairs are permitted.

4. The first time there should be a chair for every child. Then remove one or two of the chairs, depending on the number of players. When the music stops again, the children who are unable to find seats are out.

5. Continue removing several chairs each time the music stops, until there are only five players left. Then remove only one chair at a time. The player who sits in the last chair is the winner.

Note: If music is not available, begin the game by clapping loudly for the marchers. As the children are eliminated from the game, ask them to join the "clappers." The newest member of the clapping group tells the entire group when to stop by calling "Stop!" This is often better than music because it keeps all of the children busy throughout the game.

Stepping Stones

Ages: 5-11   No. of Players: 8-24

WHAT'S NEEDED?

☐ Sheet of Colored Construction Paper for Each Player
☐ Piano
OR
☐ Record Player and Records
☐ Prize

PREPARATION
None.

PRESENTATION
1. Arrange the sheets of construction paper on the floor, in as large a circle as possible. Keep the papers at least one step apart.
2. Ask the children to stand on the papers. When the music starts, they are to step to the outside of the circle. They must march around the circle without stepping on the papers.
3. When the music stops, each child must put both feet on the nearest paper.
4. After the first round, remove one or two papers each time you begin a new round. Then any child who cannot find a paper is out.
Note: This game is a good substitute for Musical Chairs when not enough chairs are available.

Under the Broom

Ages: 5-11   No. of Players: 6-15

WHAT'S NEEDED?

☐ Broom, Mop Handle, or Smooth Stick of Equivalent Length
☐ 2 Piles of Books, Each about 4' High
☐ Prize

PREPARATION
Build up the two piles of books about 3 feet apart. Lay the broom across the top of the books.

PRESENTATION
1. Ask the children to line up behind the host or hostess. The first player goes "under the broom," circles around, and walks to the end of the line.
2. Then the next player does the same. Any player who touches the broom is out. (Pony tails, sashes, and stiff petticoats do not count. Use your own judgment as to what jiggles the broom.)
3. When the child who was first reaches the head of the line again, remove a few books from each pile.
4. Continue playing, removing more books each time around, until only one player can wiggle under without touching the broom.

Elimination Contests

Do This and Add Something

Ages: 8-11   No. of Players: 6-15

WHAT'S NEEDED?

☐ Prize

PREPARATION
None.

PRESENTATION

1. Sit in a circle with the children. Ask the child on your right to make some small motion in a seated position—clapping once, touching his left toe with his right hand, or pulling his hair. The child on his right must do exactly what he did, just once.

2. Continue counterclockwise around the circle with each child exactly repeating the same motion.

3. When it is the first child's turn again, he repeats the motion he started. Then the next child must perform that same motion and add a new one. These two motions are then repeated around the circle.

4. Any child who does not perform the various motions in the correct order is out. A child is also out if he uses the wrong hand for a one-handed motion. You may wish to drop out of the game after the second round or so. You may let the children think it is to save time, but actually you will be "saving face," for this game becomes exceedingly difficult!

5. Continue around the circle, having a different player add the new motion each time. The last player to remain in the game is the winner. He really deserves his prize for he may have had to remember 10 or 15 different motions in the proper sequence!

Concentration

Ages: 9-11   No. of Players: 6-15

WHAT'S NEEDED?

☐ Prize

PREPARATION
None.

PRESENTATION

1. Sit in a circle with the children. Give each child a number in order, from one to however many children are playing.

2. Show them how to clap the following routine in unison: clap hands to knees, clap hands once together, hold right hand up and snap fingers, hold left hand up and snap fingers. It does not matter if some children cannot make a noise as they snap their fingers.

3. As soon as a rhythm is established, start the game. Call out your own number as you snap the fingers on your right hand. Call out the number of another player as you snap the fingers on your left hand. The player whose number you call must respond with his own number on the next snap of right fingers, and the number of another player on the next snap of left fingers. That player must pick it up immediately. Everyone in the circle continues to clap and snap.

4. Whoever hesitates and does not speak while snapping the proper finger, or calls a non-existent number, is out. When someone is out, all remaining players move up one number. Now everyone must remember a *new* number! Continue playing until only one player remains in the game.

Ghost

 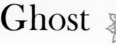

Ages: 9-11   **No. of Players: 6-10**

WHAT'S NEEDED?

☐ Prize

PREPARATION

None.

PRESENTATION

1. Sit in a circle with the children. Begin spelling a word with any letter. The next person adds another letter. If the following person cannot avoid completing the word, he becomes a G (first letter of word Ghost. The object of the game is to keep from becoming a GHOST!).

2. The next player then begins a new word. Words must have three or more letters. Letters cannot be added unless the player can state, if challenged, what word he has in mind. If a player does not believe that a word can be formed with the letters he has received, he challenges the person just before him. If the player cannot give a word, he becomes a G. Otherwise the player who challenged him becomes a G.

3. Each time a player misses, he takes on another letter—G, H, O, S, or T—until he finally becomes a "ghost." At that point he is out of the game.

4. Continue playing until all but one player have become ghosts.

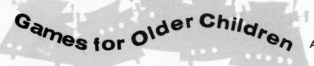

Games for Older Children

Tracing Stars

Ages: 7-11   No. of Players: 6-24

WHAT'S NEEDED?

- ☐ Cardboard
- ☐ Scissors
- ☐ Tracing Paper
- ☐ Prize

FOR EACH PLAYER:

- ☐ Sheet of Paper
- ☐ Pencil

In the beginning of the section on GAMES, there is a collection of games which are particularly well suited for the very young child. On these 20 pages you will find a group of games which have been singled out for the older children. They are not overly complex, but they do require some dexterity and concentration in order to be played successfully.

PREPARATION

Using the pattern given here, trace and cut out of cardboard one star for each player.

PRESENTATION

1. Give each child a cardboard star, a pencil, and a sheet of paper. Tell each one to find a smooth working surface (either the floor, a tabletop, or a magazine). No one is to start until you say "Go!"

2. Explain that the object of this game is to trace as many stars as possible on the sheet of paper. The stars may touch each other, but must not overlap or hang over the edge of the paper.

(A trick which some children soon discover is to have one side of a point on the star become one side of a point on another star.)

3. All players begin when you say "Go!" The child who finishes first is not necessarily the winner—it is the child with the most stars!

4. It is easier to count the stars if you number them as you count. Be lenient with wiggly lines, but do not count stars that are drawn entirely freehand.

VARIATIONS Using the patterns given here, have the children trace pumpkins for Halloween, bells for New Year's Day, hearts for Valentine's Day, or bunny heads for Easter.

Enlarge patterns by following the directions on page 8.

Map-Making

Ages: 7-11   **No. of Players: 6-18**

WHAT'S NEEDED?

☐ Colored Picture or Drawing
   Containing at Least 10 Items

☐ Prize

FOR EACH PLAYER:

  ☐ Pencil

  ☐ Sheet of Paper

PREPARATION

On a separate sheet of paper assign numbers from 1 to 10 to ten different items in the picture. Skip around: item 1 may be in the upper right-hand corner, item 2 in the center, item 3 at the left. Keep this list to use in playing the game.

PRESENTATION

1. Give each player a pencil and sheet of paper.

2. Explain that you are going to show them a picture for just one minute. During that time they are to study the picture very carefully, but they may not write anything.

3. After the children have had a chance to study the arrangement of the various items in the picture, remove it.

4. Then tell them to take their pencils and place a 1 on their papers where they think they saw the barn door (or whatever your item 1 is). Pause; then ask them to write a 2 wherever they remember seeing the mother duck (or whatever your item 2 is).

5. Continue through item 10. Then ask them to write their names in one corner. Collect the papers and check them to see who came the closest to making an exact map of the picture.

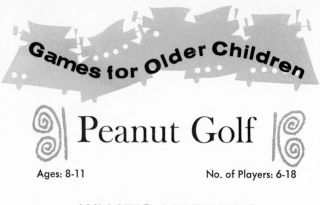

Games for Older Children

Peanut Golf

Ages: 8-11   No. of Players: 6-18

WHAT'S NEEDED?

☐ 9 Coasters
☐ 9 Small Boxes (earring boxes)
☐ Colored Construction Paper
☐ Toothpicks
☐ Scissors
☐ Cellophane Tape
☐ 3" x 5" Cards
☐ Peanuts
☐ Pencil for Each Player
☐ Prize

PREPARATION

Set up a miniature golf course in one room, or in several rooms. Use books, furniture, pots, and pans as "obstacles."

Use the coasters for tees and the small boxes for the nine holes. Cut an opening in one end of each box to make it easier to drive in the peanuts.

Cut tiny flags out of construction paper and number them from 1 to 9. Attach the flags to toothpicks with cellophane tape. Tape the flags to the boxes in a logical order around the course.

Using 3 x 5-inch cards, prepare score cards for each player. List holes 1 to 9.

PRESENTATION

1. Give each player a pencil (for a "golf club") and a score card. (The game will be more fun if you can obtain golf-club-shaped pieces to attach to the ends of the pencils. They can often be found in variety stores. They are not essential for the game, however.)

2. Explain that you will start each child at a different hole, to avoid crowding. If there are more than nine players, assign two to each hole.

3. Each push or stroke with the "golf club" counts one point. Each player must keep track of the number of strokes he uses to drive the peanut into each hole. After each hole he must write the number of strokes for that hole in the proper place on his score card.

4. After all of the children have played all nine holes, ask them to add up their scores. The child with the *lowest* score is the winner.

Human Tic-Tac-Toe

Ages: 8-11   No. of Players: 10-18

WHAT'S NEEDED?

- [ ] Colored Construction Paper
- [ ] White Construction Paper
- [ ] Scissors
- [ ] Black Crayon
- [ ] Book of Quiz Questions
- [ ] Small Prizes

PREPARATION

Cut the white construction paper into sheets approximately 4 x 5 inches. You will need one of these sheets for each player. On half of these sheets, mark a large X with the black crayon. On the other half, mark a large O.

PRESENTATION

1. Select nine sheets of paper, in neutral colors, from the pack of construction paper. Place these papers on the floor in the pattern shown above. Keep the papers about 2 feet apart.

2. Divide the group into two teams. Ask the players to stand on opposite sides of the room. Give all the members of one team sheets with X's on them to hold. Give the other team's members the sheets marked with O's.

3. Tell the children that this game is played like tic-tac-toe. You are going to ask the first child on one team a question. If he answers correctly, he can choose any paper on the floor to stand on. If a child answers his question incorrectly, he must go to the end of his team.

4. Then ask the first player on the other team a different question. If he answers correctly, he can choose a paper to stand on. The object of the game is for the players to arrange themselves so that three players of one team are standing in a row—vertically, horizontally, or diagonally. Of course, the other team will try to prevent this!

5. The first team to have three players in a row wins one game. The first team to win five games is the winning team. Give a small prize to each member of the winning team.

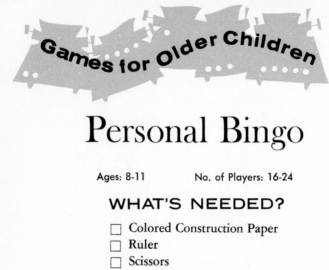

Personal Bingo

Ages: 8-11   No. of Players: 16-24

WHAT'S NEEDED?

☐ Colored Construction Paper
☐ Ruler
☐ Scissors
☐ Pencil for Each Player
☐ 3 Prizes

PREPARATION

For each player, rule off a sheet of construction paper, as shown below. Using any colors, cut four smaller pieces of paper for each player.

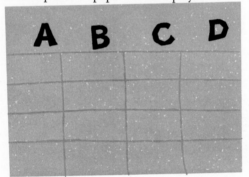

PRESENTATION

1. Give each player a pencil, four small papers, and one of the ruled sheets of construction paper.

2. Ask each player to write the letters A, B, C, and D—one at the top of each small paper. Then ask them to write their names beneath each of these letters.

3. Collect the small papers from each player. Shuffle them well and hold them while the players prepare the large sheet.

4. Ask the players to write the names of the children at the party in the 16 boxes on the large sheets. They must use each name only once; they must not copy each other's papers.

If there are more than 16 children, all the names will not be used by each child. If there are fewer than 16 at the party, make up additional names. (Be sure to add four small papers apiece for each of these made-up names.)

5. Tell the children that this game is a form of Bingo. Instead of calling numbers, you will call the letter of the column and a player's name.

6. Without looking, pull out one of the small papers you have been holding. Call out "B, Shirley." Instruct the children to put a check in the proper box, if they have this name in this column on their papers. Then call out the next one, "D, Jim."

7. For ease in checking later, place the small papers down in separate piles for A, B, C, and D.

8. The first child to have four checks in a row—across, up and down, or corner to corner—is the winner of the first game.

9. Check this child's paper. If it is correct, shuffle all the little papers together before starting a second game.

10. For the second game, tell the children to ignore their check marks. This time they are to mark their boxes with an X. For a third game, ask the children to circle each box. Give a prize to the winner of each game.

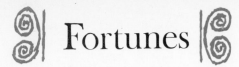

Fortunes

Ages: 8-11   No. of Players: 6-18

WHAT'S NEEDED?

- ☐ Carbon Paper
- ☐ Typewriter (if available)
- ☐ Typing Paper
- ☐ Pencil for Each Player

PREPARATION

For each player, prepare a sheet of paper with the following headings on it. Use carbon paper (and a typewriter, if available) to make your task easier.

Name
Boy's or Girl's Name
Year
Number
Color
Another Color
Job
Place
Game

PRESENTATION

1. Give each child one of these sheets of paper and a pencil. Ask them to write their names and wait for further instructions. Do not tell them the name of the game, for they might then force their answers to your questions.

2. Ask them to write answers to each of the following questions. Give one line at a time and wait until all have finished that line.

Boy's or Girl's Name—"If you are a boy, write a girl's name, but not your sister's. If you are a girl, write a boy's name, but not your brother's. If you know the last name, write that too."

Year—"Write the number of any year—this year, or 1776, or 2025, or any year in the past or future."

Number—"Write any number you like from one to a million."

Color—"Write the name of any color. If you have trouble spelling one like lavender or fuchsia, I'll help you."

Another Color—"Write a different color this time."

Job—"Write any job you would like to have."

Place—"Write the name of any place, anywhere in the world."

Game—"Write the name of any game you enjoy playing."

3. Collect the papers and pencils. Then tell the children that the game they have been playing is called Fortunes. Each child has just written his own fortune.

4. You are going to read the papers aloud. What each child has written will tell the following story:

Boy's or Girl's Name—Whom the child will marry, or did marry.

Year—When they will marry, or did marry.

Number—Of children.

Color—The eyes of all of their children.

Another Color—The hair of their children.

Job—Job child writing the paper will have when he or she is grown up.

Place—Where this couple will live.

Game—That they will play all day long.

One of the fortunes might sound like this: "Mary married Bobby in 1952. They have 7,539 children with purple eyes and chartreuse hair. Mary is a ballet dancer. They live in Alaska, and play jump rope all day long."

There is no prize given for this game. Just reading aloud the fortunes is fun enough for everyone.

Games for Older Children

Memory Teaser

Ages: 9-11   No. of Players: 6-24

WHAT'S NEEDED?

- ☐ Paper and Pencil for Each Player
- ☐ Cellophane Tape
- ☐ Prize
- ☐ Tray with 21 Small Items, Such as:
  - ☐ Lollipop
  - ☐ Domino
  - ☐ Band-Aid
  - ☐ Safety Pin
  - ☐ Paper Clip
  - ☐ Bobby Pin
  - ☐ Crayon
  - ☐ Button
  - ☐ Mirror
  - ☐ Pen
  - ☐ Battery
  - ☐ Penny
  - ☐ Spoon
  - ☐ Key
  - ☐ Empty Match Folder
  - ☐ Empty Cellophane Tape Reel
  - ☐ Small Ball of Wool
  - ☐ Jack
  - ☐ Comb
  - ☐ Marble
  - ☐ Pencil

PREPARATION

Arrange the 21 items on the tray. Tape them in place.

PRESENTATION

1. Give each child a pencil and a sheet of paper. Ask each child to write his name and the numbers from 1 to 21 on the paper.

2. Ask the children to put their pencils down. Tell them that they must not write again until you have removed the tray to another room.

3. Carry the tray around so that each child has a good opportunity to study the items on it. Then remove it. Tell the children to write down all the items they can remember.

4. When the children pause and begin to chew their pencils, it is time for another peek at the tray. Again no child may write until the tray is removed.

5. Allow a few more minutes, and then collect the papers. Read aloud the paper with the longest list so that the group may listen for duplications or mistakes. The winner is the player whose paper has the most correct items.

Burglary

Ages: 9-11　　　　　　　　**No. of Players: 6-18**

WHAT'S NEEDED?

☐ Paper and Pencil for Each Player
☐ Additional Sheets of Paper
☐ Cellophane Tape
☐ Prize

PREPARATION

Tear a sheet of paper into small pieces—one for each player. Mark each piece with a large number, from one up to the number of players.

PRESENTATION

1. As the guests arrive, take each one aside and ask him to lend you an article belonging to him— a glove, a bracelet, tie pin, or boot. Ask him not to tell anyone else what he has loaned you.

2. Place his item on a table with one of the numbered papers taped to it. Do not arrange the items in the order of the guests' arrivals. Be sure to include an item from the birthday child as well.

3. Write down the number and owner of each item on another sheet of paper, for use as an answer sheet.

4. After everyone has arrived, give each player a pencil and a sheet of paper. Ask each one to write his name and the numbers from 1 to 12 (if that is the total number of players) on the paper.

5. Explain that there has been a robbery, but luckily the stolen articles have been found. It is now necessary to identify the owners of the stolen goods.

6. Ask the players to study the items displayed in "Exhibit A." They are then to write the names of the owners they have decided upon next to the corresponding numbers on the papers.

7. Let them work on this for a while. They may study each other to see who is missing an article of clothing or jewelry.

8. Ask them to give you their papers as they finish. The first child finished with the most correct answers is the winner.

Quick Change

Ages: 9-11　　　　　　　　**No. of Players: 6-18**

WHAT'S NEEDED?

☐ Paper and Pencil for Each Player
☐ Prize

PREPARATION

None before the party.

PRESENTATION

1. Ask the children to inspect the room thoroughly.

2. Then have them adjourn to another room to have refreshments or to play another game.

3. While they are gone, make 10 or 12 changes in the appearance of the room—move a chair, close a book, open a window.

4. Write down these changes as you make them, for later use as a check list.

5. When the children return, give each of them a pencil and paper. Ask them to write down any changes in the room that they notice. It is not necessary to tell them how many changes were made.

6. After about 10 or 15 minutes, collect the papers and see who was the most observant.

Games for Older Children

Identifying Months

Ages: 9-11   No. of Players: 6-24

WHAT'S NEEDED?

☐ Colored Construction Paper
   (twelve 9″ x 12″ sheets)
☐ Scissors
☐ Paste
☐ Old Magazines
☐ Pencil and Paper for Each Player
☐ Prize

PREPARATION

Thumb through old magazines to find appropriate pictures to represent each month of the year. Some suggestions are:

January—a clock, small baby, or snow scene.
February—valentine, hatchet, log cabin.
March—shamrocks, lion and lamb, kite flying.
April—Easter eggs, rainy-day scene.
May—flowers, parade, a mother.
June—a bride, father, or graduate.
July—fireworks, American flag.
August—swimming scene, picnic scene.
September—schoolroom, school bus.
October—Columbus' ships, Halloween motifs.
November—election placards, Pilgrims, turkey.
December—any Christmas scene or motif.

Cut out one picture for each month. Mount the pictures on sheets of construction paper. Write the numbers from 1 to 12 under each picture in random order.

Then prepare answer sheets for each child. On each sheet list the months in order, one beneath the other. Draw a blank line next to each month.

PRESENTATION

1. Give each child a pencil and one of the previously prepared sheets of paper. Ask the children to write their names on their papers.

2. While they are doing this, place the twelve pictures around the room in obvious places.

3. Hold up one picture for the group to work out together—preferably the one representing the current month. Tell the children to write the number appearing on this picture next to the correct month on their papers.

4. Permit the children to work in any order. The first one finished with the most correct answers is the winner. If the child who finishes first has eight correct answers, wait to see if someone else figures out 10, or possibly 12, before awarding the prize.

Who Am I?

Ages: 9-11   No. of Players: 6-18

WHAT'S NEEDED?

- ☐ Ball of String
- ☐ Scissors
- ☐ Colored Construction Paper (one 9" x 12" sheet for each player)
- ☐ List of Storybook Characters, Movie Stars, or Television Performers (one for each player)
- ☐ Prize

PREPARATION

Cut strings long enough to go over the children's heads. Fasten one string to each sheet of construction paper to make a placard. Print a different name from your list on each placard.

PRESENTATION

1. This game is a good party-opener. As each child arrives, hang a placard around his neck, with the name dangling down his back.

2. After each child has received his placard, you may announce the category—movie stars, storybook characters, or TV performers.

3. Each player then goes from one to another, asking questions that can be answered "Yes" or "No" until he discovers what name is on his back.

4. Watch to see that no one peeks over his shoulder, or tries to read his placard in a mirror! The first one to come to you with his "name" guessed correctly is the winner.

Games for Older Children

Smell It!

Ages: 9-11   No. of Players: 6-18

WHAT'S NEEDED?

- ☐ 10 Small Brown Pill Bottles
- ☐ Adhesive Tape
- ☐ Scissors
- ☐ Paper and Pencil for Each Player
- ☐ Prize

Small Quantities of Following Liquids:
- ☐ Perfume
- ☐ Vinegar
- ☐ Calamine Lotion
- ☐ Water
- ☐ Orange or Prune Juice
- ☐ Liquid Soap
- ☐ Spirits of Camphor
- ☐ Mouthwash
- ☐ Cough Medicine
- ☐ Merthiolate

PREPARATION

Label the bottles from 1 to 10 with small pieces of adhesive tape. Fill each bottle about half full. Make an answer sheet for yourself, listing which liquid was placed in which bottle.

PRESENTATION

1. Give each child a piece of paper and a pencil. Ask the players to write their names and the numbers from 1 to 10 in a column on the left.

2. While they are doing this, place the bottles in safe places around the room. Warn the children not to pick up the bottles. Some of the liquids might stain if spilled.

3. Instead, ask the children to lean over each bottle, smell, and try to guess what is in it. They must write their answers in the appropriate spaces on the papers.

4. Keep track of the order in which the children finish. (Set a time limit of about 10 or 15 minutes.) Then collect the papers and tell the children what was in each bottle.

The first child finished with the most right answers is the winner. Spelling does not count. This is a very difficult game, and the winner might not guess more than five correctly.

Hear It!

Ages: 9-11   No. of Players: 6-18

WHAT'S NEEDED?

- ☐ A Few Dried Beans in a Pill Bottle
- ☐ A Few Pins in a Pill Bottle
- ☐ Deck of Cards
- ☐ Cellophane
- ☐ Ball-point Pen
- ☐ Large Zipper
- ☐ 2 Buttons
- ☐ Roll of Scotch Tape
- ☐ Piece of Elastic, about 12″ x 1″
- ☐ Scissors
- ☐ Paper and Pencil for Each Player
- ☐ Screen (optional), or Large Box
- ☐ Prize

PREPARATION
None.

PRESENTATION

1. Give each player a piece of paper and a pencil. Ask the players to write their names and the numbers from 1 to 10 in a column on the left side of the paper.

2. If you have a screen, set up the 10 items listed above behind it. If not, place them in a large box and stand with it behind the children.

3. Announce the number of each item. Shake, shuffle, crumple, click, zip, knock, tear, snap, or cut with each item.

4. Without looking at you, the children are to write down what they think is making each noise.

5. Collect the papers and show the children how you made the noises. The child with the most correct answers is the winner.

Feel It!

Ages: 9-11 **No. of Players: 6-18**

WHAT'S NEEDED?

- ☐ 12 Squares of Dark Cloth, 12" x 12"
- ☐ 12 Rubber Bands
- ☐ Adhesive Tape
- ☐ Scissors
- ☐ Paper and Pencil for Each Player
- ☐ Prize

12 Small Objects, Such as:
- ☐ Art Gum Eraser
- ☐ Flashlight Battery
- ☐ Paper Clip
- ☐ Safety Pin
- ☐ Garter
- ☐ Lipstick Container
- ☐ Roll from Inside of Cellophane Tape
- ☐ Hard Candy
- ☐ Bobby Pin
- ☐ Roller Skate Key
- ☐ Marble
- ☐ Penny

PREPARATION

Place one object in each square of cloth. Wrap up and fasten with a rubber band. Label each package with a number from 1 to 12, using adhesive tape. Make a check list for yourself.

PRESENTATION

1. Give each player a pencil and a piece of paper. Ask the children to write their names and the numbers from 1 to 12 in a column on the left.

2. While they are doing this, place the 12 packages around the room.

3. Tell the children that they are to go around the room and handle each package. Without opening any of the packages, they are to guess the contents of each. They must write their answers in the appropriate spaces on their papers.

4. Keep track of the order in which the children finish. The first child finished with the most correct answers is the winner.

5. Collect all the papers and open the packages to show the children the contents. The paper clip and safety pin are often confused. And many times the children can't tell whether the money is a dime or a penny!

Games for Older Children

Post Card Identification

Ages: 9-11   No. of Players: 6-18

WHAT'S NEEDED?

- ☐ 12 Picture Post Cards
- ☐ Masking Tape
- ☐ Scissors
- ☐ Paper and Pencil for Each Player
- ☐ Prize

PREPARATION

If you have a number of well-known landmarks in your town or area, choose a series of 12 local post cards. If not, you may choose famous shots of New York City, national monuments, or Washington, D.C.

Use the tape to mask out any identifying information on both sides of the post cards. Number the cards from 1 to 12.

PRESENTATION

1. Give each child a sheet of paper and a pencil. Ask the children to put their names and the numbers from 1 to 12 in a column on the left side of the paper.

2. While they are doing this, place the 12 post cards around the room. Space them so that the children may view them easily.

3. Tell the players to walk around and study the scenes on the cards. They are to write what each card pictures in the appropriate space on their sheets of paper.

4. Keep track of the order in which the children finish. The first child finished with the most correct answers is the winner. (Spelling does not count.)

Novelty Competition

Ages: 9-11 (Girls)   No. of Players: 6-18

WHAT'S NEEDED?

- ☐ Sheet of Paper and a Pencil for Each Player
- ☐ Tape Measure
- ☐ Index Card
- ☐ Prize (optional)

PREPARATION

Prepare one sheet of paper for each player that reads as follows:

Name
1._____
2._____
3._____
4._____
5._____
6._____
7._____
8._____
9._____
10._____
Total _____

Then, using the index card, prepare an "answer sheet" for yourself indicating the children's attire and appearance and the point values as follows:

1. **Dress or blouse:** plain—1, plaid—3, print—5
2. **Shoes:** black—1, red—3, any other color—5
3. **Socks:** white—1, colored—3
4. **Hair:** Pony tail—1, pigtails—2, long (loose)—3, short—5
5. **Number of petticoats:** 1 point each
6. **Belt:** bow—1, buckle—2, button—3 no belt—5
7. **Necklaces, rings, bracelets, watches:** 1 point each
8. **Number of inches around waistline:** measure for each child
9. **Number of month of child's birthday:** January (1st month) to December (12th month)
10. **Number of day of child's birthday**

PRESENTATION

1. Give each girl a piece of paper and a pencil.

2. Inform the group that this game is all about them. Tell the children that they will receive points for their clothing, appearance, and "personal history." No changes in costume may be made from this moment until the end of the game.

3. Ask each girl to write her name at the top of her paper. Then read one item aloud at a time and assist the children in deciding how many points that item is worth to each. After each girl has written her own score for that item, go on to the next. You will have to measure their waistlines yourself; be sure to count half inches!

4. At the end of the game, help the players total their points. The girl with the highest score is the winner.

Categories

Ages: 9-11   **No. of Players: 6-15**

WHAT'S NEEDED?

☐ Ruler
☐ Paper and Pencil for Each Player
☐ Prize

PREPARATION

Make a copy of the chart below for each player. Do not fill in the boxes under the letters C, A, R, D. Use plain white paper or construction paper.

PRESENTATION

1. Give each player a pencil and one of the previously prepared sheets of paper.

2. Explain that the children are to fill all the boxes without looking at each other's papers. They are to think of unusual words beginning with the letters heading the various columns, for their scores depend on choosing words which other players do not have.

3. When the children have finished, each player will score his own paper. Ask the first child on your right what his food beginning with the letter C is. Anyone else with this same word must raise his hand. Count the number of raised hands. Each of these players must write the total number in the box with this first word.

If no one else has the same word, the player reading aloud writes a zero in the first box.

4. Continue counterclockwise around the circle. Each player has an opportunity to present his food beginning with the letter C, if it has not already been presented by another player.

5. After the foods beginning with the letter C have been scored, go on to the next column. After all 16 boxes have been scored, ask the children to add up their points. The child with the *lowest* score is the winner.

	C	A	R	D
FOODS	Celery 4	Artichoke 6	Raspberry	Doughnut 2
GIRLS' NAMES	Cecile	Alexandra	Robin	Denise
BOYS' NAMES	Chester	Allon	Robert	David
PLACES	Chicago	Afghanistan	Rhodesia	Denmark

 Typewriter

Ages: 10-11   No. of Players: 14-20

WHAT'S NEEDED?

- ☐ Unruled Index Cards
- ☐ Red and Blue Crayons
- ☐ 2 Rubber Bands
- ☐ Small Prize for Each Member of One Team (optional)

PREPARATION

If you expect *14 players,* take 14 index cards and write the following letters *once each* in red and *once each* in blue on separate cards:

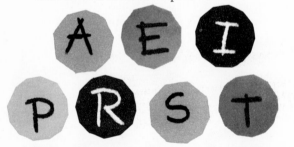

Pile the red letters together and fasten with a rubber band. Do the same with the blue letters.

Then copy the following list on another index card for your use during the game. The seven letters are used at least 14 times each:

1. stripe	9. respite	17. past
2. aster	10. pair	18. tape
3. trip	11. tries	19. site
4. parts	12. spare	20. spat
5. stair	13. tears	21. spire
6. sprite	14. ripe	22. rasp
7. east	15. seat	23. airs
8. pirates	16. pier	24. pies

If you expect *20 players,* take 20 index cards and write the following letters *once each* in red and *once each* in blue on separate cards:

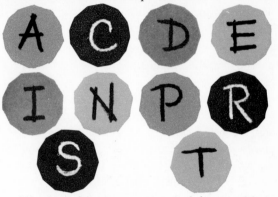

Pile the red letters together and fasten with a rubber band. Do the same with the blue letters.

Then copy the following list on another index card for your use during the game. The 10 letters are used at least 11 times each:

1. cried	9. trend	17. drip
2. paint	10. sped	18. nest
3. stride	11. scant	19. crane
4. carts	12. aster	20. detain
5. prince	13. price	21. spice
6. sprain	14. dent	22. aired
7. stand	15. pace	23. depict
8. aspic	16. train	24. spaced

PRESENTATION

1. Divide the group into two teams and stand them, facing each other, on opposite sides of the room.

2. Designate one team as the Red Team. Give each member an index card with a letter written in red. The other team becomes the Blue Team. Give out the cards with blue letters so that the order down the line corresponds exactly with that of the Red Team. If you have more children than cards, arrange for two children to share one card.

3. Stand in the middle of the room at the head of both teams. Explain that you are going to read a word from your card. The players who are holding the letters which make up that word must rush to the front of the room and arrange themselves in the correct spelling order. Thus, the remaining players must be able to read the word from left to right.

Demonstrate by using the word "Step." In the picture below, the Red Team on the left has spelled the word correctly. The members of the Blue Team on the right have their letters completely jumbled! This is one game in which spelling *does* count.

4. Read one word at a time. Watch closely to decide which team forms the word the fastest. Score one point for the first team to form each word correctly. Play for a final score of 11 points.

5. If prizes are given for this game, all members of the winning team should receive a small prize.

RED TEAM   BLUE TEAM

Spell It

Ages: 9-11 **No. of Players: 2-24**

WHAT'S NEEDED?

☐ Ruler
☐ Pencil and Paper for Each Player
☐ Prize

PREPARATION

On each paper, draw a square containing 25 boxes. Each box should measure ½ inch x ½ inch.

PRESENTATION

1. Give each player a pencil and one of the previously prepared sheets of paper. Sit down with the children in a circle.

2. Explain that each player, in turn, will name one letter of the alphabet. The object of the game is to form words with the letters as they are given.

3. Every player must write every letter as it is spoken. The letters may be placed in whatever box each player thinks is best for him. Wait until everyone has written the letter before going on to the next player.

4. No player may erase a letter after the game begins. Explain that, for scoring purposes, one-letter words do not count. Proper nouns, abbreviations, and contractions also do not count. Words can be spelled vertically as well as horizontally. Letters may be used in more than one word.

5. After all 25 boxes have been filled in, ask the children to sign their names and hand in their papers for scoring. You will need to score each paper yourself. During this time the children can play another game that does not require your full attention.

SCORING Give one point for each letter in each word: 5-letter word, 5 points; 4-letter word, 4 points, and so on. Below are examples to guide you in scoring. Both of these children wrote down the same letters, but their arrangements are quite different. The child with the highest score is the winner.

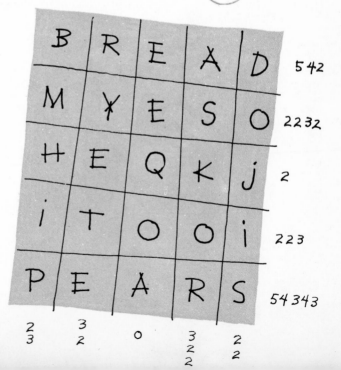

Scrambled Animals

Ages: 10-11   No. of Players: 6-24

WHAT'S NEEDED?

☐ Paper and Pencil for Each Player
☐ Prize

PREPARATION

Prepare a paper with the following list for each player:

Name——————————————

ZOO RESIDENTS

1. onli ————————————
2. neeltaph ————————————
3. yeknom ————————————
4. accopek ————————————
5. lagominf ————————————
6. seroorinch ————————————
7. grite ————————————
8. areb ————————————
9. photopsuimap ————————————
10. esla ————————————
11. almla ————————————
12. riffgea ————————————
13. okoranga ————————————
14. cloordice ————————————
15. unpinge ————————————

Then prepare an answer sheet for yourself as follows:

1. lion	9. hippopotamus
2. elephant	10. seal
3. monkey	11. llama
4. peacock	12. giraffe
5. flamingo	13. kangaroo
6. rhinoceros	14. crocodile
7. tiger	15. penguin
8. bear	

PRESENTATION

1. Give each child a copy of the scrambled animals' names and a pencil.

2. Emphasize the fact that spelling *does* count in this game. The first child to unscramble the most names correctly is the winner. You may set a 10- or 15-minute time limit on this game.

Advanced Fortunes

Ages: 10-11   No. of Players: 6-18

WHAT'S NEEDED?

☐ Paper and Pencil for Each Player

PREPARATION

On each paper, duplicate the following list.

Name: Another Color:
Boy's or Girl's Name: Job:
Year: Place:
Number: Game:
Color:

PRESENTATION

1. Ask the children to sit down in a circle. Give each player a pencil and one of the previously prepared papers. Ask them to write their names on the first line. Do not tell the name of the game, in order to avoid forced answers.

2. On the second line ask them to write a G if they are girls, a B if they are boys. Then ask them to fold down the papers so that just their names are covered.

3. Collect the papers and mix them well. Pass out the papers again.

4. Now ask the children who have G's to write a *boy's* name next to the G. Ask those who have B's to write a *girl's* name next to the B. Then have them fold down the papers to cover that line and pass the papers one child to the right.

5. Fold and pass for each new item on the list. After they have all filled in the space "Game," collect the papers again.

6. Read the papers aloud individually, according to the following pattern:

"Michael married Melinda in 1956. They have 6,749 children with pink eyes and green hair. Since he is a jockey, they live in Hawaii. They play jump rope all day long."

7. No prize is necessary for this game. Just being the recipients of some wild and farfetched fortunes is reward enough.

Name: Michael
Boy's or Girl's name: (B) Melinda
Year: 1956
Number: 6,749
Color: Pink
another Color: Green
Job: Jockey
Place: Hawaii
Game: Jump Rope

Cartoon Captions

Ages: 10-11   No. of Players: 6-15

WHAT'S NEEDED?

- ☐ 6 Cartoons
- ☐ Colored Construction Paper
- ☐ Cellophane Tape
- ☐ Scissors
- ☐ Pencil and Paper for Each Player
- ☐ Prize

PREPARATION

Cut out six cartoons from newspapers or old magazines. Cut off the "punch lines." Mount the cartoons on sheets of construction paper. Using large figures, number these cartoons from 1 to 6.

Prepare answer sheets for each of the players, using the following form:

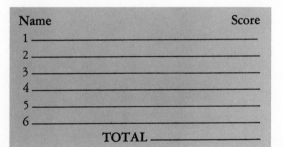

Name	Score
1 _____	_____
2 _____	_____
3 _____	_____
4 _____	_____
5 _____	_____
6 _____	_____
TOTAL	_____

PRESENTATION

1. Show the children the six cartoons you have prepared. Point out that in each case the "punch line" (or caption) is missing. (You may wish to show them some other cartoons so that they all understand exactly what a "punch line" is.)

2. Give each player a pencil and one of the previously prepared sheets of paper. Ask them to write their names on the papers.

3. While they are doing this, place the cartoons around the room. You may wish to secure them with cellophane tape.

4. Then explain that you would like the children to supply the "punch lines" for these cartoons. They are to walk around the room and study the cartoons in any order. As they decide on an appropriate caption, they are to write it in the space corresponding to the number on the cartoon.

5. When everyone is finished, collect the papers and sit down in a circle with the children. Shuffle the papers and explain that you are going to read aloud all the answers twice.

6. First read through all the punch lines (or captions) for Cartoon No. 1. Tell the children to listen for the one they like best. During the second reading they are to vote for the caption they think is best for each cartoon. No one may vote for his own.

7. Ask the children to raise their hands to vote. Mark the number of votes in the score box after each caption. When you have read all of the captions for all six cartoons, total up the scores. The player with the highest score is the winner.

Rotative Games

A whole party may be built around the rotative games described on these six pages. Or you may wish to include a group of them with other games during a long party.

Each game takes about 10 minutes to play, plus an additional three minutes to score each game and change to the next. Groups of three or four children play one game at a time. The same children move as a group to the next game.

Rotative Games

Ages: 9-11   **No. of Players: 12-32**

WHAT'S NEEDED?

FOR EACH GROUP:

- ☐ Card Table and Chairs (optional)
- ☐ Pads and Pencils (for scoring individual games)
- ☐ Index Cards
- ☐ Prize or Prizes

Note: Additional items are listed under each game.

If you decide to use four games, set up four tables (if available) or corners. The games remain in the same positions throughout the game period. The players rotate from table to table.

Prepare a score card for each player. Use index cards and mark them as shown below.

```
Name ..............
Game 1 ...........
Game 2 ...........
Game 3 ...........
Game 4 _____
     Total ........
```

Whatever game a player plays first is Game 1 for his score card.

Explain the rules and scoring systems for all the games before the children begin to play. Then you will only need to arbitrate disputes and call the time. At the end of the game period you may wish to award a prize to the child with the highest score in each group. Or you may award a grand prize to the child with the highest score of all, if the groups are equal in size.

Toothpick Balance

WHAT'S NEEDED?

☐ Round Toothpicks
☐ Pill Bottle

PREPARATION
None.

PRESENTATION
1. Ask each player to take 10 toothpicks. The first player balances one toothpick across the open neck of the bottle. The next player balances one of his toothpicks alongside or on top of the first.

2. The third player adds one of his to the pile. The game continues around the table until one player causes his own toothpick or any others to fall. He must then add all the fallen toothpicks to his pile. The next player begins again.

3. The game is over when one player succeeds in getting rid of all of his toothpicks. Score 10 points for this player. The player with the fewest number of toothpicks scores 5; the player who comes in third scores 3. The player with the most toothpicks left scores zero.

4. If the other tables haven't finished their games yet, tell the children to divide up the toothpicks and play again. The more games they can fit in, the higher their scores.

RULES	
When You Roll:	Draw:
6	Body
3	Head
1	Eyes
5	Feelers
2	Tail
4	One Set of 4 Legs
	(Two Sets Are Needed)

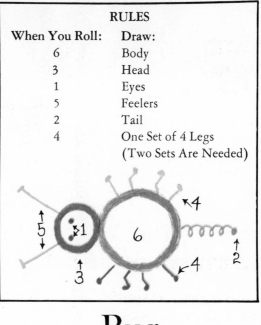

Bug

WHAT'S NEEDED?

☐ Pair of Dice (use only one)
☐ Paper and Pencil for Each Player
☐ Index Cards

PREPARATION
Using index cards, make a copy of the rules (above) for each player.

PRESENTATION
1. The object of this game is to draw as many Bugs as possible, according to the rules. No player may start a second Bug until the first one is completed.

2. Each player in turn rolls the dice, trying first for a 6. Once a player rolls a 6, he may draw the body. After he has drawn a body, he may add a head when he rolls a 3, a tail when he rolls a 2, or four legs on one side when he rolls a 4. Once he has drawn the head, he may add eyes when he rolls a 1, and feelers when he rolls a 5.

3. When you call time, the player with the most Bugs scores 10; the player with the second highest number of Bugs scores 5; the player who comes in third scores 3; the player with the lowest number of Bugs scores zero. In the case of a tie, parts of Bugs may be counted in scoring.

Rotative Games

Horse Race

WHAT'S NEEDED?

- ☐ Deck of Playing Cards
- ☐ 4 Pennies
- ☐ Tracing Paper
- ☐ Paper and Pencil
- ☐ Ruler
- ☐ Black and Red Crayons

PREPARATION

Make a "race track" by ruling off a sheet of paper into four columns vertically and 13 boxes horizontally, as shown here:

Finish Line

Using tracing paper, transfer the outline of the horse into the first box in each column. Draw a red diamond, black club, red heart, and black spade on the saddles, as shown. Mark in the Finish Line.

PRESENTATION

1. Ask each player to choose a horse and place his penny at the top of that column. Ask one player to serve as dealer and shuffle the cards.

2. The dealer takes off one card at a time from the top of the pack. As he calls out the suit, the player who has chosen that suit moves his penny one box toward the finish line. Whoever crosses the finish line first is the winner of that game. Another child becomes the dealer. The players may keep the same horses or switch suits.

3. When you call time, whoever has won the most races scores 10 points; the second winner scores 5; the third scores 3; and the lowest scores zero.

Bingo

WHAT'S NEEDED?

☐ Bingo Set

PREPARATION

None.

PRESENTATION

1. Ask one player to act as caller. The group proceeds to play Bingo.

2. When you call time, whoever has won the most games scores 10 points; the second winner scores 5; the third scores 3; and the lowest scores zero.

Marble Roll-Away

WHAT'S NEEDED?

☐ Shoe Box
☐ 3 Marbles
☐ Scissors
☐ Crayons

PREPARATION

Cut and label a shoe box as directed on page 61.

PRESENTATION

1. Explain that each player in turn will roll the three marbles, one marble at a time. Have the starting line the same for all players. One game consists of three rounds. Tell the children to play quickly to fit in as many games as possible.

2. When you call time, the player who has won the most games scores 10 points; the second winner scores 5; the third scores 3; the lowest, zero.

Put and Take

WHAT'S NEEDED?

☐ Uncooked Red Kidney Beans
☐ Put and Take Top

PREPARATION

None.

PRESENTATION

1. Ask each player to take 10 beans. Also place 10 beans in the center of the table. Each player in turn will spin the top. These tops are usually labeled "Put all," "Take all," "Put one," "Take one," "Put three," "Take three," "Put four," "Take four."

2. The first player spins the top and takes or puts in as many beans as directed by the top. The players continue spinning around the circle until time is called.

If one player should win all the beans before the time is up, tell the group to keep playing. They should also continue if there are no beans in the center. Sooner or later someone will have to put in some beans.

3. When you call time, the player with the most beans scores 10 points; the second winner scores 5; the third winner scores 3; and the lowest, zero.

Rotative Games

Dots and Boxes

WHAT'S NEEDED?

☐ Paper and Pencil for Each Player

PREPARATION

Prepare a series of papers with six rows of six dots each, as shown below. Space the dots about ½ inch apart. Make enough papers so that each group will have at least two.

PRESENTATION

1. Explain that each player in turn may draw one line, horizontally or vertically, to connect two dots. The object of the game is to form as many boxes as possible, without giving the other players the opportunity to form boxes.

2. When three lines have been drawn to form three sides of a box, the next child may draw the line to make the fourth side. He puts his initial in the center of the box and goes again. He may keep going until he is unable to claim any more boxes. He must then draw another line anywhere on the diagram, even if it means giving the next player a box or group of boxes.

3. There are 25 boxes to be won in each game. Two games may be played within the time limit.

4. When you call time, the players should add up their total number of boxes won in the two games. The player having the most boxes scores 10 points; the second winner scores 5; the third scores 3; and the lowest, zero.

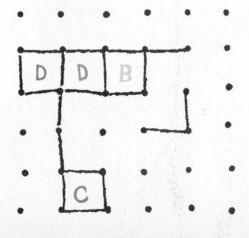

Bowling

WHAT'S NEEDED?

☐ 10 Dominoes
☐ Small Rubber Ball
☐ Paper and Pencil

PREPARATION

Set the dominoes up on a sheet of paper in a triangular pattern. Mark the pattern on the paper, as shown below, so that the dominoes will always be replaced in the same positions.

PRESENTATION

1. Explain that each game consists of three rounds. During each round each player has two chances to knock down all 10 dominoes. If he succeeds on the first chance, he receives 20 points and does not need his second chance. If he needs two chances, his score is the total knocked down, with a maximum of 10. A player should not set up the dominoes again between his first and second chances.

2. When you call time, the player with the highest total score rates 10 points; the second winner, 5 points; third, 3 points; and lowest, zero.

Hangman

WHAT'S NEEDED?

☐ 4 Index Cards
☐ Large Piece of Paper and Pencil for Each Player

PREPARATION

List one of the categories given below on one side of the four index cards. On the other side list the eight items which correspond to each category.

PRESENTATION

1. Tell the first player to draw a card. Without letting the others see his card, he chooses a word from his list of items.

2. On his paper, he draws a gallows and enough dashes for each letter of his word.

3. He names the category, and then the other players take turns guessing the word, one letter at a time. If the letter guessed appears in the word, he must write it in the correct space. If the letter appears more than once, he writes it in as many times as it appears.

4. If the letter does not occur in the word, the player must write it on the side of his paper so it won't be used again. For each incorrect guess, the player draws a portion of a man on the gallows: head, body, first arm, second arm, first foot, second foot.

5. If a player guesses a word before it is completely filled in, that player wins. Or if the player whose turn it is manages to hang a man completely before the word is guessed, that player wins.

6. The game continues around the circle until time is called. Each time the players choose a different word from their lists.

7. When you call time, the player with the most wins scores 10 points; the second winner scores 5; the third winner scores 3; the lowest, zero.

CATEGORIES

Means of Travel	School	Medicine	Jobs
1. escalator	1. classroom	1. stethoscope	1. exterminator
2. motorcycle	2. textbook	2. ambulance	2. doctor
3. buggy	3. examination	3. fluoroscope	3. counselor
4. cruiser	4. promotion	4. hypodermic	4. housekeeper
5. sedan	5. instructor	5. anesthetic	5. shoemaker
6. elevator	6. gymnasium	6. operation	6. grocer
7. rocket	7. vacation	7. appendectomy	7. veterinarian
8. scooter	8. student	8. tonsillectomy	8. dancer

On these 16 pages you will find a mixed group of games. They are not hunts, games of skill, or relay races. There are some for the younger children, some for the older children, and some which fit a wide age range.

Leaf through this group carefully. You will be sure to find two or three games to round out the selections you have already made from the other sections of this book.

Surprise Package

Ages: 5-11   No. of Players: 6-15

WHAT'S NEEDED?

- ☐ Shoe Box
- ☐ 2 Pieces of Plain Wrapping Paper
- ☐ 1 Piece of Decorated Wrapping Paper
- ☐ Rope
- ☐ 1 Package of Chocolate Bits or Candy Corn
- ☐ Cellophane Tape
- ☐ 1 Pair of Large Mittens
- ☐ 1 Dull Knife
- ☐ 1 Fork
- ☐ 1 Sandwich Bag for Each Player

PREPARATION

Wrap the package of chocolate bits or candy corn in one piece of plain wrapping paper. Then wrap again in the second piece of plain paper. Place this package in the shoe box. Cover the box with the decorated paper. Tie the box with rope, making a loose knot with many loops.

PRESENTATION

1. Sit down with the group in a circle. Place the Surprise Package in front of you with the fork on the left, the knife on the right, and a mitten on each side. Keep the sandwich bags handy.

2. Explain that this is not a gift for the party child, for who would bring a gift tied with rope! No, it is a surprise for all of the children. When it is opened, each child will receive something from this package. However, no one may attempt to open the package unless he is wearing the mittens and holding the knife and fork.

3. Set the equipment in front of the first child. When you say "Go!" he must put on the mittens, pick up the knife and fork, and go to work on the knot. Meanwhile, the group counts slowly from one to 10. At 10, he must stop, put down the knife and fork, take off the mittens, and pass everything to the next child. At the word "Go!" the second player continues to unwrap the package from the point where the first player stopped.

4. As the rope, gift paper, shoe box, and inner wrappings are undone, remove them from the game area. The mittens, knife, and fork must be used until the candies are uncovered.

5. Reach for the chocolate bits (or candy corn) quickly. Spread the last piece of wrapping paper on the floor and scatter about 20 pieces of candy on it.

6. Explain that each child will receive some of the candies as his prize. The amount depends on how lucky each one is today.

7. Give a sandwich bag to the child whose turn is next. Tell him to turn around and hide his eyes. Choose a child about halfway around the circle and ask him to point to one of the candies. Everyone except the child hiding his eyes knows which candy has been chosen.

8. Ask the child to open his eyes. He may then pick up one candy at a time until he touches the candy that was chosen. Then everyone calls out "Stop!" and he gets no more candies. (Even if it happens to be the first candy he touches, he must stop. But be sure to slip him a few candies anyway at the end of the game.)

9. If the first player picks up all, or almost all, of the candies, scatter a few more on the paper before the next player hides his eyes.

10. Continue playing until all of the children have had a chance to pick up candies and to select the "Stop!" candy. A second round of the game, much as the children may clamor for it, would be boring to them. Instead, suggest a bag blowing and bursting session after all the candies are gone—if it hasn't already been done!

Miscellaneous Games

Magic Circles

Ages: 5-11   **No. of Players: 6-18**

WHAT'S NEEDED?

☐ Colored Construction Paper
☐ Luncheon Plate
☐ Scissors
☐ Rubber Band
☐ Prize

PREPARATION

Select a different color paper for each player. Using a luncheon plate for a pattern, cut out one circle of each color. Also cut four or five 1-inch squares of each color. Mix the squares and fasten with a rubber band.

PRESENTATION

1. Place the colored circles on the floor. Ask each child to choose a circle and stand on it.

2. Stand in front of the group with the packet of colored squares. Without looking, draw out one of the squares. Give it to the child who is standing on the matching circle.

3. Draw three or four colored squares and then call out "Change!" The children keep the squares they already have, but select a different circle to stand on.

4. After another three or four squares, call "Change!" again. Repeat until you have given out all your squares of paper.

5. Ask the children to count the number of squares they have collected. The child who has the most squares is the winner.

Note: If you cannot find a different color for each player, use two circles of each color. Then when you draw out a colored square, tear it in half. Give each child with a matching circle one of the halves. Emphasize that these halves each count as a whole at the end of the game.

Choosing Colors

○ ◎ ◍ ○ ○ ○ ◎ ○ ○ ◎ ○ ◎ ○ ○ ◎ ◎ ○

Ages: 5-11   No. of Players: 6-15

WHAT'S NEEDED?

- ☐ Index Cards
- ☐ Crayons (a different color for each player)
- ☐ Scissors
- ☐ 2 Rubber Bands
- ☐ Prize

PREPARATION

Cut the index cards in half so that you have five halves for each player. (For the remainder of the game, each half will be referred to as a "card.")

Choose a different color for each group of five cards. With crayon, color just a small area in the center of each card.

Make two piles of cards. One pile will contain one card of each color; the other pile, four of each color. Shuffle the pile of cards containing four of each color. Fasten each pile with a rubber band.

PRESENTATION

1. Ask the children to sit down in a circle. Give each child one card from the thinner pack of cards.

2. Spread the cards from the thicker pack, face down on the floor, in the center of the circle. The object of the game is to be the first child to hold all five cards of the same color.

3. Go around the circle counterclockwise. The first child takes one card from the center and compares it with his card. If it is the same color, he may keep it. If it is not exactly the same color, he must place it face down in the center of the circle again. If another child happens to see his color on a card which is being replaced, he must remember the position of the card until it is his turn.

4. After you have a winner (the first child to hold five cards of the same color), ask the other children to turn up the cards nearest them. Then they can see where their particular cards were hidden.

Note: You may wish to play a simpler version with groups of five-year-olds and large groups of six-year-olds. Place only two cards of each color in the center of the circle. Then the child who first holds three cards of the same color wins.

Shoe Scramble

○ ○ ○ ○ ○ ○ ◎ ○ ○ ◎ ○ ○ ○ ◎ ○

Ages: 5-11   No. of Players: 6-15

WHAT'S NEEDED?

- ☐ Piece of Chalk
- ☐ Prize

PREPARATION

Mark each child's initials on the bottom of the soles of his shoes. Then collect all the shoes. Scatter them along one side of the room.

PRESENTATION

1. Ask the children to line up on the opposite side of the room.

2. At the word "Go!" they are to try to find both shoes, put them on, and return to the starting line. The first child back is the winner—if he is wearing his own shoes!

Chip Change

Ages: 6-11   No. of Players: 6-24

WHAT'S NEEDED?

☐ Red, White, and Blue Poker Chips
☐ 2 Small Bags
☐ Pencil and Paper, for Scoring

PREPARATION

Multiply the number of players by two and add six to your answer. Divide this number by three to see how many chips of each color will be needed. For instance, for 12 children you would multiply 12 x 2 (24); add 6 (30); divide by 3 (10 red, 10 white, 10 blue).

Place two chips of each color in one small bag. Place the remaining chips in the other bag and mix thoroughly.

PRESENTATION

1. Sit in a circle with the children. Give each child two chips of different colors from the bag with the most chips in it: red and white, blue and white, or red and blue. Do not give them two of the same color, for they are less apt to receive a point that way.

2. Pick up the first bag and show the children that it contains two white, two blue, and two red chips. Explain that you are going to reach into the bag without looking and pull out two chips. Whoever has exactly that combination of colors will receive one point. If two or three players have the same combination, they each receive one point. If no one has that combination, you will replace the chips and pull out two more.

3. Before you actually begin to play, make out a score sheet. Write down the names of the children in the order in which they are seated. Also announce what score will win the game, since it would not be fair to decide this after the game is underway. Play for 7 points with six- to eight-year-olds; 10 points for nine- to 11-year-olds.

4. After you have scored the first round and replaced your chips in your bag, show the group how to change chips. The children will probably want to *exchange* them, but for this game a different method is used.

When you call "Change!" each child is to pick up one of his chips in his right hand and drop that chip into the lap of the child on his right.

Many young children have trouble distinguishing right from left, especially when seated opposite other children in a circle. Ask them to raise the hand which they use to salute the flag. Most of them will raise their right hands automatically.

5. This new chip may or may not be the same color as the one a child already holds. Reach into your bag and begin calling out new combinations of chips. When you finish this round, call out "Change!" again. Play until someone reaches the winning score.

VARIATIONS For parties which come during the holidays, vary the color combinations of the chips. Use a 50-cent piece for a pattern, and cut the "chips" out of construction paper.

Easter: pink, blue, yellow
Halloween: orange, black, white
Christmas: red, green, white

Crazy Auction

Ages: 7-11   **No. of Players: 6-15**

WHAT'S NEEDED?

- [ ] 20 Small Objects (suggestions given on this page)
- [ ] Shoe Box
- [ ] 20 Index Cards
- [ ] Prize

FOR EACH PLAYER:

- [ ] 10 Dried Beans
- [ ] Sandwich Bag

PREPARATION

Collect the 20 small objects and place them in a shoe box. Write the name of each object and its point value on an index card.

Count out 10 beans for each player and place them in the sandwich bags.

PRESENTATION

1. Ask if any of the children have ever heard of or been to an auction. If not, give some background information. Explain that the man in charge, or auctioneer, holds up one item at a time and asks who wants to buy it. You can't always tell by looking at something how valuable it is. Often something that looks very precious will turn out to be a piece of junk when you get it home. The item that is being auctioned off goes to whoever offers the most money—the highest bidder.

2. Now give out the sandwich bags filled with dried beans. Explain that each bean is worth one dollar. Therefore, each child has $10 to spend, and no more!

3. Begin the auction by holding up one item from the shoe box. Ask who would like to buy it. Suggest that the children start their bidding with one dollar so that they won't waste their money if no one else wants that particular item. Give everyone an opportunity to bid. Close the bidding on each object by saying, "Going, going, gone." Give the object to the highest bidder, and collect in beans the number of dollars he has bid.

4. After all of the objects have been sold (or after all the money has been spent), give each bidder the index cards containing the point values for his items. Remind the children that this is a "Crazy Auction." Thus, the objects which they might consider very valuable may have very low point values.

5. Help each child to add and subtract his points for a grand total. The winner is the player with the largest number of points.

An Empty Lipstick Container
6 points

A Wrapped Hard Candy
2 points

A Small Stick
5 points

A Small Ball of Wool
4 points

A Paper Fastener
3 points

A Dead Flashlight Battery
9 points

A Piece of Cardboard
3 points

A Tiny Empty Box
5 points

A Bracelet
Subtract 10 points

A Peanut
Subtract 5 points

A Crayon
Subtract 3 points

A Marble
Subtract 1 point

A Safety Pin
1 point

A Paper Clip
2 points

A Band-Aid
3 points

A Key
8 points

A Shoelace
6 points

A Comb
1 point

A Bobby Pin
4 points

A Small Rock
6 points

Memory Lotto

Ages: 7-11   No. of Players: 6-12

WHAT'S NEEDED?

- ☐ Same Materials as for Picture Lotto, page 38
- ☐ Prize

PREPARATION

If you do not have two different sets of Picture Lotto on hand, you can make your own sets by following the directions on page 38.

PRESENTATION

1. Sit with the children in a circle. Place one large card, face down, in front of each player. Explain that no one may look at this card until you give the signal.

2. When you say "Go!" the children are to turn the cards over and memorize the pictures on the card and the positions of these pictures.

3. After about one minute, tell the children to turn the cards face down again and *sit on them*. (They are going to duplicate the positions on the larger card with smaller cards as the game is played. Therefore, it is less confusing if the larger card is completely out of sight.)

4. Hold up one small card at a time. Whoever remembers having that card may request it and must place it on the floor in front of him. As the players add several cards, they must try to arrange them to correspond with their original cards.

5. The first child to arrange six cards in perfect order is the winner. The children will probably want you to continue playing the game to see how well each one remembered.

Bingo

Ages: 7-11   No. of Players: 6-24

WHAT'S NEEDED?

☐ Bingo Set
☐ Colored Construction Paper
☐ Scissors
☐ Prizes

PREPARATION

Check your Bingo set to be sure that you have enough cards for each player, a checking sheet, a complete set of numbers, and a handful of cover slips for each player. If you do not have enough cover slips, you can make them out of construction paper. Use a penny for a pattern.

PRESENTATION

1. Settle each player with a card and a handful of cover slips. Play several rounds of ordinary Bingo, in which the winner is the first child to cover a row horizontally, vertically, or diagonally.

2. Clear the cards after each round. Let the children change their cards occasionally. To stimulate further interest, let the winners be the first ones to cover their cards in some of the variations shown below. The winner of the last game might be the first one to cover his whole card.

BINGO VARIATIONS

OUTSIDE SQUARE

H-SHAPE

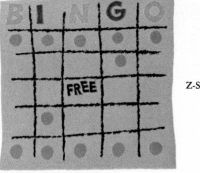

Z-SHAPE

Double It

Ages: 7-11   No. of Players: 6-15

WHAT'S NEEDED?

☐ Index Cards
☐ Crayons
☐ Rubber Band
☐ Prize

PREPARATION

Choose any 12 letters of the alphabet. Using different colors for each letter, make six cards bearing each letter. Shuffle the cards thoroughly and fasten with a rubber band.

PRESENTATION

1. Sit in a circle with the children. Ask them to help you place all the cards, face down, in the center of the circle.

2. On the first round, everyone takes one card and keeps it. On the second round, each player hopes to match this card with another card bearing the same letter. If the two cards make a pair, the player places the pair, face up, in front of him and draws another card. If the cards do *not* make a pair, the player replaces the card he has drawn and waits for the next round.

3. If a player decides that the card he is holding is not "lucky," on his next turn he may announce, "I am going to change my card." He exchanges his card for a new card. He must then wait another turn before trying for a pair.

4. The first person to complete three pairs of cards is the winner.

Magic Boxes

Ages: 7-11 **No. of Players: 6-32**

WHAT'S NEEDED?

- ☐ Colored Construction Paper or Gift Wrapping Paper
- ☐ Ruler
- ☐ Scissors
- ☐ Prize (optional)

PREPARATION

Cut out as many 6-inch squares of colored paper as you have players. For this particular game, you are going to make the Magic Boxes for the children ahead of time. Just fold and cut according to these seven easy steps.

Step 1: Fold one square in half diagonally both ways. Press each crease with your fingernail. Open flat.

Step 2: Fold all four corner points—A, B, C, and D—into the center point E. Open flat.

Step 3: Fold A to I and open, B to H and open, C to G and open, D to F and open.

Step 4: Fold A to F and open, B to G and open, C to H and open, D to I and open.

Step 5: Cut out the eight triangles marked X, as indicated by the solid black lines. Make additional cuts as indicated by the solid black lines shown on the diagram.

Step 6: Fold J and K into L; M and N into O. Do not open.

Step 7: Bring point C through point R and open on the other side. Put point A through point P and open. Your box is now tightly closed.

PRESENTATION

1. Group the boxes together and ask each child to select a box.

2. Tell the children that these boxes were put together very carefully and that they are extremely difficult to open. Challenge them to open the boxes without tearing the paper.

3. You may wish to give a prize to the first child who succeeds without damaging his box.

Note: If you are playing this game with a group of 10- or 11-year-olds, they may wish to go on and make some boxes themselves. Have an extra supply of 6-inch squares on hand for this purpose. Additional uses for these Magic Boxes are given on pages 136-137.

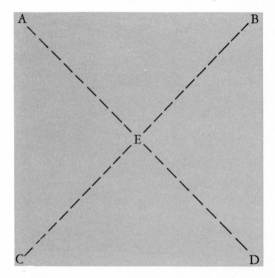

STEP 1

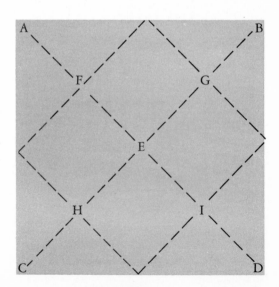

STEP 2

MAGIC BOXES

Follow these step-by-step diagrams to make the Magic Boxes described on page 134. Dotted lines represent fold lines; heavy black lines, cut lines.

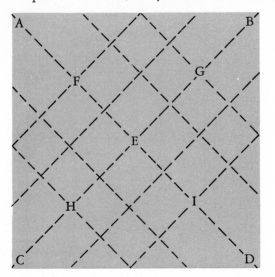

STEP 3

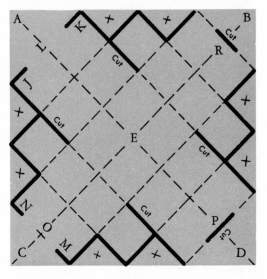

STEP 5

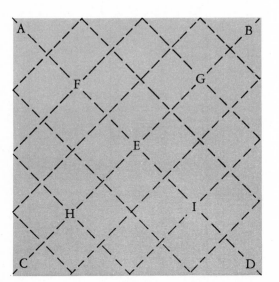

STEP 4

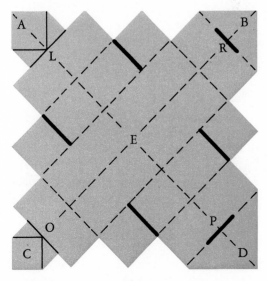

STEP 6

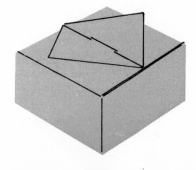

STEP 7

Miscellaneous Games

Puzzle Boxes

WHAT'S NEEDED?

- [ ] Colored Construction Paper or Gift Wrapping Paper
- [ ] Ruler
- [ ] Scissors
- [ ] Jigsaw Puzzles (see page 60)
- [ ] Prize

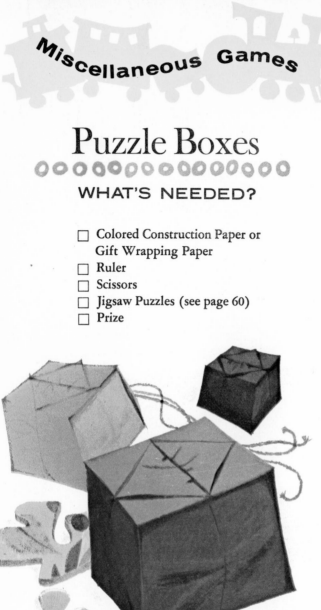

PREPARATION

Following the directions on page 134, make one Magic Box for each player.

Prepare Jigsaw Puzzles according to the directions on page 60. Before closing the boxes, put one set of puzzle pieces in each box.

PRESENTATION

Give out the Magic Boxes and explain the rules for putting together the puzzles, as described on page 60. Before the children can begin to solve the puzzles, however, they must figure out how to open the boxes!

Favors

WHAT'S NEEDED?

- [ ] Colored Construction Paper or Gift Wrapping Paper
- [ ] Ruler
- [ ] Scissors
- [ ] Tiny Candies

PREPARATION

Following the directions on page 134, make one Magic Box for each guest. Before closing the boxes, fill them with tiny candies: cinnamon drops, candy corn, chocolate bits.

PRESENTATION

Use the boxes as favors on the table, or give them out to the children at the end of the party for their "take-home" bags.

Strings in Magic Boxes

WHAT'S NEEDED?

- [ ] Colored Construction Paper or Gift Wrapping Paper
- [ ] Ruler
- [ ] Scissors
- [ ] Ball of String
- [ ] Prizes (optional)

PREPARATION

Cut one length of string for each player. Vary the lengths from 1 inch to 2 feet.

Following the directions on page 134, make one Magic Box for each player. Insert one string in each box before closing the boxes.

PRESENTATION

1. Group the boxes together and ask each child to select one box. Tell them to open the boxes very carefully.

2. Ask them to compare the lengths of their strings to see who has the longest and who has the shortest. Prizes may be given to these two players.

Stunts in Magic Boxes

Ages: 8-11 (Girls)   No. of Players: 6-15

WHAT'S NEEDED?

- ☐ Colored Construction Paper or Gift Wrapping Paper
- ☐ Ruler
- ☐ Scissors
- ☐ 3" x 5" Pad
- ☐ Prize (optional)

PREPARATION

Choose one stunt for each player from the following list. Copy the stunts onto separate sheets from the small pad.

Following the directions on page 134, make one Magic Box for each player. Insert one stunt in each box before closing the boxes.

PRESENTATION

1. Arrange the boxes in a group and ask each player to select one box. Tell the girls to open their boxes carefully, so that no one else sees their stunts.

2. Allow each girl one turn in which to act out her stunt. She may not have any help in acting out the various parts of her stunt. However, it need not be done in pantomime.

3. You may wish to have the children vote for the best performance. Give each child two votes. Then perhaps they will vote not only for their best friends but for the best performers, too. You may wish to give a prize to the child who receives the highest number of votes.

STUNTS

1. Pretend that you are getting ready to go to a party.
2. Pretend that you are at the movies and can't see over the heads of those in front of you.
3. Pretend that you are at the zoo and want to take home a monkey.
4. Pretend that your little brother has just broken your favorite record.
5. Pretend that you are shopping and can't decide which dress to buy.
6. Pretend that you are on a crowded bus and can't find a seat.
7. Pretend that you are at the store and can't find the list you thought you had taken to tell you what to buy.
8. Pretend that you are a mother and your child doesn't want to go shopping with you.
9. Pretend that you are late for school.
10. Pretend that you are trying to teach your parakeet to say your name.
11. Pretend that you are a teacher and your class talks too much.
12. Pretend that your dog is getting soap suds all over the house.
13. Pretend that you are in a strange city and no one speaks your language.
14. Pretend that you are on a picnic and suddenly it begins to rain and thunder.
15. Pretend that you have to wait on a long, long line.

Five of a Kind

Ages: 7-11   No. of Players: 8-24

WHAT'S NEEDED?

☐ Light-colored Construction Paper (3 sheets of one color)
☐ Black Crayon
☐ Scissors
☐ Ruler
☐ Rubber Band
☐ Prize

PREPARATION

Divide the construction paper into 1½-inch squares. Place a large number 1 in the center of five of the squares, a large number 2 in the center of five more squares, and continue to make five squares of each number up to the maximum number of guests expected.

Cut out the squares and pile them up in groups of five, with the number-1 squares on the bottom of the pile. Fasten with a rubber band.

PRESENTATION

1. Count the number of children who will be playing the game. If there are 12, use only the groups of squares from 1 to 12. Discard the others. Shuffle the pile of squares thoroughly.

2. Give out five squares to each player. Check to be sure that no child receives more than two squares with the same number. Tell the children not to show their cards to any other player.

3. Explain that the object of the game is to end up with "five of a kind." Keeping the number side hidden, they are to trade one square at a time. When a child receives a card that matches one in his hand, he keeps it and places it next to the mate. He then walks around the room with another card held out, face down, looking for a trade.

4. Caution the children not to ask for the numbers they need, for their opponents will be sure to withhold those cards. If a player should hold three number-8 squares and two number-4 squares at one time, it would be wiser for him to trade one of the number-4 squares, since he has fewer of these.

5. The first child who comes to you with "five of a kind" is the winner.

Snap Words

Ages: 8-9   No. of Players: 6-12

WHAT'S NEEDED?

- ☐ Index Cards
- ☐ Bright-colored Crayon
- ☐ Rubber Band
- ☐ Prize

PREPARATION

Take a package of index cards and print the following letters of the alphabet as directed:

B (*Make 5 cards*)	**M** (*Make 7 cards*)
C (*Make 5 cards*)	**N** (*Make 4 cards*)
D (*Make 4 cards*)	**P** (*Make 8 cards*)
F (*Make 4 cards*)	**R** (*Make 9 cards*)
G (*Make 4 cards*)	**S** (*Make 9 cards*)
H (*Make 4 cards*)	**T** (*Make 5 cards*)
L (*Make 5 cards*)	**W** (*Make 4 cards*)

Draw a line under each letter so that there will be no confusion between such letters as M and W. Shuffle the letters thoroughly and fasten with a rubber band.

PRESENTATION

1. Sit facing the group of children. Explain that you are going to announce a category and then flash a card. The object of the game is to call out as quickly as possible a word in that category beginning with the letter you are holding up. Whoever "snaps out" the word first receives the card.

2. Use the same category 10 or 12 times before changing to another category. Suggested categories are clothing, furniture, boys' names, girls' names, colors, games, foods.

3. If you cannot decide who called out a word first, replace the card in the pack and go on to the next letter. If a child calls out a word that has already been used, do not give him a card.

4. When you have used up all of the letters, the child holding the most cards is the winner.

Miscellaneous Games

4. Give each child one turn and then play two more rounds. Total the value of the gold for each player to find the best gold digger!

Gold Digging

Ages: 9-11   No. of Players: 6-15

WHAT'S NEEDED?

☐ Large Map of the United States
☐ Cellophane Tape
☐ Colored Construction Paper
☐ Tracing Paper
☐ Scissors
☐ Blindfold
☐ Pencil and Paper, for Scoring
☐ Prize

PREPARATION

Count the letters in the name of each state and write that number next to the name of the state on the map. If you prefer, trace and cut out of construction paper 50 "bags of gold." Write the numbers on the bags and tape them to the map.

Tape the map to the wall so that it will be at shoulder height for most of the children.

PRESENTATION

1. Tell the players that they will be prospecting for gold in the United States. The value of the gold to be found in each state is equal to the number of letters in the name of that state. Contrary to our history, the players will soon find that it is not wise to head West for gold!

2. Ask the children to form a single line. Write the names of the children on your score sheet in the same order. Draw three columns after the list of names.

3. Establish a starting line about six feet in front of the map. Blindfold the first child. Turn him about gently three times and head him toward the map. Tell him to point directly ahead with one finger. Whatever state he first touches is the state where he is prospecting for gold. Record the value of his "gold" on the score sheet.

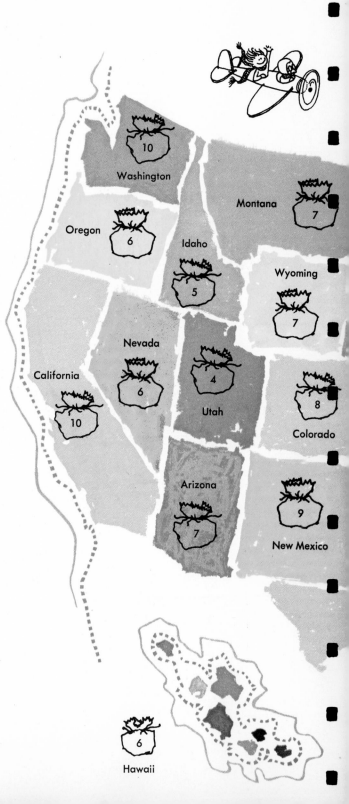

Alaska 6

Pattern for Bag of Gold 12

New Hampshire 12
Vermont 7
Maine 5
Massachusetts 13
N. Dakota 11
Minnesota 9
Wisconsin 9
Michigan 8
New York 7
Rhode Island 11
S. Dakota 11
Iowa 4
Connecticut 11
Nebraska 8
Illinois 8
Indiana 7
Ohio 4
Pennsylvania 12
New Jersey 9
Delaware 8
Kansas 6
Missouri 8
Kentucky 8
W. Virginia 12
Virginia 8
Maryland 8
Oklahoma 8
Arkansas 8
Tennessee 9
N. Carolina 13
Texas 5
Mississippi 11
Alabama 7
Georgia 7
S. Carolina 13
Louisiana 9
Florida 7

Adaptations for Handicapped Children

Children who have physical or mental disabilities are, first and foremost, children, with the need for color and excitement and surprise in their lives. They have friends, and should be able to entertain their friends. The child who is giving the party may invite friends who have similar disabilities and also friends, brothers, sisters, and cousins who do not have these disabilities.

Parties for children who are blind or deaf or confined to bed or wheel chair are not only possible, but necessary for normal social development. It is strongly recommended that the number of guests invited for children who are below par physically be limited to two or three, and certainly not more than six. Children with long-term disabilities, such as blindness or deafness, or braces, who are otherwise healthy, may invite twelve guests most comfortably. Retarded children should have small parties, with guests who are close to their mental age levels, or who understand the necessity for playing simple games.

PARTIES FOR CHILDREN WHO ARE BLIND OR PARTIALLY SIGHTED

A parent who has learned to accept and cope with the problems of her child's blindness may still be uneasy at the thought of entertaining a group of blind children, or of her child's competing with sighted children at a party. This fear may be compensated for by carefully planning each detail in advance.

It is better if the children have had a chance to visit and explore your home before the party, but it is not mandatory. If the children do not know your home, remove from the rooms in which the children will play and eat as much furniture as possible. If the children are familiar with your arrangement of furniture, do not change it until after they have arrived. Set the table so that each child's plate and favors are directly in front of him. Include all the standard items of party fun: candy baskets, hats, and a favor—or string leading to a Jack Horner pie. Snappers may frighten younger children. Use paper plates and cups to avoid unnecessary concern on a child's part if anything is accidentally knocked off the table.

Be careful when the group moves from one room to another that no one is left behind in a strange room. Have an extra person available to guide guests to the bathroom.

Choose as quiet a room as possible in which to play. When you are leading the games, do not attempt to out-shout the youngsters. They may become noisy while getting their bearings in an unfamiliar place. Games which involve as many players as possible at one time are important.

Choose games such as Candy Hunt, Chip Change (with circles, squares, and triangles instead of colored chips), Grandmother's Club, Crazy Auction, Under the Broom, and Murder! (with heavy cardboard cards, on one of which you have taped an open safety pin for a "lethal weapon," to indicate the murderer, and on two of which there are buttons, to "sew up the case" for the detectives). String Maze, Stringing Straws, Twenty Questions, Boots without Shoes, Telephone, and Time! are also good choices.

PARTIES FOR CHILDREN WHOSE MOVEMENTS ARE LIMITED

Adaptations of activities may be made according to the area and severity of the disability. Some children may be limited in the ability to move from place to place, but have the full use of their hands. The activities for these children will eliminate hunts and races and consist of games of skill such as Feeding the Elephant, Paper Toss, Marble Roll-Away, Stringing Straws, puzzles, writing games, rotative games, guessing games, and other circle games. It may be necessary to arrange chairs and tables for play if comfortable positions cannot to be found on the floor. During refreshment time, food may be served on individual tables or card tables if seating arrangements cannot be planned around one table.

Other youngsters may lack the muscle control necessary for handling small items. There should be nothing breakable for them to handle, and sufficient space at the table for favors so that an extraneous movement will not dislodge them. Games involving thinking and speaking will have to be emphasized over those requiring motion, but games with colorful equipment should be included. For example, Crazy Auction could be adapted so that the children would not have to handle the beans, but could spend their "money" from a large, previously prepared chart.

Sometimes children are confined to bed with noncommunicable diseases and are able to have a few friends in to celebrate an occasion. Children in wheel chairs may have or attend parties. Such parties should have few guests and be very short.

PARTIES FOR CHILDREN WHO ARE MENTALLY RETARDED

Children who are six or seven years old chronologically, but only three or four mentally, will be happiest at the unorganized type of party recommended for young children, where they receive their gifts, eat ice cream and cake, and play with a few selected toys. The older child can play the group games that are recommended for children of his mental age level, emphasize participation for all, and recognize his short attention span.

Brothers and sisters and playmates of average mental ability will be quite willing to participate in activities they have outgrown to make the mentally retarded child's party pleasant for him.

PARTIES FOR CHILDREN WHO ARE DEAF OR HARD-OF-HEARING

Most games are adaptable for use with children who are deaf or hard-of-hearing. Avoid those games which have complicated directions, require verbal response, or involve reading and writing beyond a very simple level for children who may not yet have facility with words. Be sure you have the attention of the group before attempting to explain the game with words and gestures.

It is easier to conduct the games in circle formation where every person can see every other person. Remember, however, that children cannot sit too long and need to move around. Many hunts, races, and contests, such as One Out, Under the Broom, and Do This and Add Something, are good for this purpose. Games of skill, such as Feeding the Elephant, Paper Toss, Marble Roll-Away, Stringing Straws, and Tracing Stars, are easily understood. Choosing Colors, Chip Change, Magic Circles, Card Trading, Odd or Even, Picture Lotto, and Memory Lotto are good for most ages. The many rotative games require concentration but are particularly good for older groups.

The usual plans may be made for refreshment time. Blowers and snappers and all the regular decorations and favors are fine.

Creative Fun

The activities on these six pages are designed for a quiet period during the party. This might come just after the refreshments have been served and just before the children are ready to go home. Children almost always enjoy making things. And they will be doubly proud to tell their families after the party, "I made it myself."

These activities require very few materials and are planned for children between the ages of 7 and 11.

TURKEY'S COMB

Enlarge patterns by following the directions on page 8.

PIG'S TAIL

Tape

Tape

Tape

Tape

Barnyard Finger Puppets

WHAT'S NEEDED?

- ☐ Colored Construction Paper
- ☐ Scissors
- ☐ Tracing Paper
- ☐ Cellophane Tape
- ☐ Crayons
- ☐ Pencils
- ☐ Rubber Cement
- ☐ Absorbent Cotton (for Lamb)
- ☐ Cardboard

PREPARATION

Using tracing paper, make a cardboard pattern of each of the animals shown here. Collect enough scissors, paper, crayons, and tape for the number of guests at your party.

Make up one or two of the puppets in advance to have on hand as samples.

PRESENTATION

1. Show the children one of the sample finger puppets and how it works. Ask them to choose which of the puppets they would like to make, and pass out the patterns accordingly. (Some children may have to wait their turn, and some may want to make more than one puppet.)

2. Spread out the materials on a large table. First show the children how to trace around their patterns on colored paper. Then have them add features with crayon, pencil, cotton, and cut paper.

3. When they have all finished coloring the puppets, show them how to tape the bases together to fit the size of their fingers.

4. When they each have a puppet, it is time for an impromptu puppet show, with lots of barnyard noises in the background. A good starter would be several rounds of "Old MacDonald Had a Farm," with each child taking the part of the animal he has chosen for his puppet.

Enlarge patterns by following the directions on page 8.

CHICK'S BEAK

LAMB'S EARS

Tape

Creative Fun

The large gold pattern on the next page is the starting point for making all kinds of gay party hats and table favors. When cut out of bright paper and taped together, its cone shape suggests all sorts of possibilities. We have shown three here, and doubtless your party guests will think of many more.

Party Hats and Table Favors

WHAT'S NEEDED?

- ☐ Tracing Paper
- ☐ Cardboard
- ☐ Scissors
- ☐ Pencils
- ☐ Colored Construction Paper
- ☐ Shiny Wrapping Paper
- ☐ Cellophane Tape
- ☐ Rubber Cement
- ☐ Absorbent Cotton
- ☐ Crayons
- ☐ Ribbon or Cord
- ☐ Stapler

PREPARATION

Assemble all of the suggested supplies. Be sure to have extra scissors, pencils, and small bottles of rubber cement on hand.

Make up some samples in advance, so that the children will have some idea of what they are going to make.

Prepare enough cardboard patterns so that several children can be working at the same time.

PRESENTATION

1. Spread out the supplies on a large table. Show the children the examples you have prepared ahead of time. Depending on the theme of the party, they will decide whether to make jolly Santas, polka-dotted clowns, or fancy party hats.

2. Show the children how to trace around the cardboard shape on colored paper. Have them cut out the shapes.

3. Then show them how to roll the shapes into a cone and tape them together. Once they have made the cone shapes, they can be finished in a variety of ways.

POLKA-DOTTED CLOWNS Using pennies and dimes as patterns, cut large polka dots out of colored paper. Glue them in place on the clown's body. Cut a hat out of colored paper, using the pattern given on the next page. Cut a circle for the clown's head out of colored paper. Add the features with crayons. Remind the children that each clown's "make-up" is different.

Glue the hat on the clown's head, and glue or tape the head on the body. Cut a neckpiece out of colored paper and pleat it as shown. Tape the neckpiece under the clown's chin.

The clowns can be used as table decorations at a circus party if they are made before the refreshments are served.

JOLLY SANTAS Make the cones of red paper. Cut triangular hats of red paper also. Make large black buttons, using dimes for a pattern. Glue on absorbent cotton for Santa's beard and fur trim.

Put in Santa's eyes, nose, and mouth with crayons. Staple a cord to the back of Santa's neck and he becomes a gay Christmas ornament for each guest to take home for his own tree.

GAY PARTY HATS Make a cone of double thickness by gluing together a sheet of shiny paper and one of construction paper.

Encourage the children to use their imaginations in decorating these hats. Strips of cut paper, plastic straws, sequins, artificial flowers, polka dots—all of these can be glued or taped to the hats.

Cut cord or ribbon in 18-inch lengths. Staple in pairs on the hats so that the children can tie the hats under their chins. See the pattern below.

CLOWN'S HEAD

CLOWN'S NECKPIECE

Fold on dotted lines

**CLOWN'S BODY AND
PARTY HAT PATTERN**

Enlarge patterns by following the directions on page 8.

Creative Fun

Almost all children enjoy eating lollipops, but girls in particular will have fun designing outfits for lollipop dolls. Have a good supply of the materials suggested below, and put your guests to work. They may wish to duplicate the ballerina, wild-haired witch, or posy-topped dolls shown here. Chances are, however, that they will come up with even more spectacular costumes for their lollipop dolls.

Jolly Lollipops

WHAT'S NEEDED?

- ☐ Lollipops
- ☐ Scissors
- ☐ Cellophane Tape
- ☐ Rubber Cement
- ☐ Colored Crepe Paper
- ☐ Colored Construction Paper
- ☐ Sequins, Buttons
- ☐ Wool
- ☐ Ribbon
- ☐ Artificial Flowers
- ☐ Paper Doilies
- ☐ Pipe Cleaners
- ☐ Prizes (optional)

PREPARATION

Collect the suggested materials and keep them together in a large box until the day of the party. Make up a few sample lollipop dolls to show the children.

PRESENTATION

1. Settle the children on the floor or around a large table. Give out the lollipops. Ask the children to share the tape and scissors.

2. Place the crepe paper, construction paper, wool, doilies, and other supplies in one central place. It is a good idea to have a large carton or wastebasket nearby for discarded scraps.

3. Show the children the sample lollipops you have prepared. It might be fun to have a contest to see whose doll is the prettiest, the funniest, or the most original. The children themselves may think up the categories for judging. If there are adults present who have not watched the children make the dolls, ask them to judge the finished products.

4. In addition to the fun of creating the costumes, each guest has the added pleasure of taking her lollipop doll home.

Jingle Bells

WHAT'S NEEDED?

☐ Roll of Aluminum Foil
☐ Small Paper Cup and Tiny
    Bell for Each Guest
☐ Scissors
☐ Colored String

PREPARATION

Cut the aluminum foil into pieces large enough to cover the cups. Cut the string into 8-inch lengths.

PRESENTATION

1. Give each child a piece of foil, a paper cup, a piece of string, and a tiny bell.

2. Tell the children to thread the strings through the bells and knot them. Make a double knot about 1 inch above the bell.

3. Then have the children cover their cups with foil. They will have to crease it at the top of the cup to make it fit smoothly.

4. Poke a hole with a pencil point in the bottom of each cup through the foil. Thread the string up through the hole from the inside of the cup to the outside. Tie another double knot on the outside of the cup so that the string cannot slip through the hole again.

When everyone has finished his bell, try singing a chorus of "Jingle Bells" with these shiny, jingly bells as an accompaniment.

As in the case of the Jolly Santas on page 146, these bells may be taken home to hang on each child's own tree.

Party-Giver's Check List

The following check list has been prepared to show you what steps are necessary in order to ensure a successful, smoothly run party.

You will note that not all of the steps come *before* the party. After the party is over, you may want to jot down some notes which will make your next party that much easier. And the last step of all—sending out thank-you notes. Even the youngest child can be encouraged to participate in this important aspect of his party.

BEFORE THE DATE OF THE PARTY

TWO WEEKS

☐ Decide on date, time, guests, theme, activities, refreshments
☐ Prepare invitations with child's help

TEN DAYS

☐ Send out invitations
☐ Plan activities
☐ Plan refreshments
☐ Plan favors, decorations, prizes
☐ Discuss party manners with child

ONE WEEK

☐ Purchase game materials not already on hand
☐ Purchase nonperishable items, including prizes, favors, decorations, etc.
☐ Order perishables (cake, ice cream), if necessary
☐ Check on replies to invitations
☐ Prepare games
☐ Prepare "take-home" bags for guests

ONE DAY

☐ Clear area for games
☐ Collect several large cartons for wastepaper, wrappings, etc.
☐ Clear space for guests' outer clothing
☐ Clear space for presents, prizes
☐ Prepare final guest list
☐ Purchase perishable items, except for cake and ice cream
☐ Go over party manners with child

ON THE DAY OF THE PARTY

MORNING

- ☐ Place supplies necessary for games in convenient spot
- ☐ Set table and put up decorations
- ☐ Prepare nonperishable foods
- ☐ Set out prizes, favors, "take-home" bags
- ☐ Remove pets
- ☐ Pick up ice cream and cake (if ordered)

WHEN GUESTS ARRIVE

- ☐ Arrange for young host or hostess to greet guests at door and accept presents graciously
- ☐ Hang up guests' outer clothing
- ☐ Begin activities—games, entertainment, creative fun
- ☐ Serve refreshments
- ☐ Give out "take-home" bags and favors
- ☐ Say good-by to guests with child

AFTER GUESTS LEAVE

- ☐ Clean up
- ☐ Look over presents with child
- ☐ Provide relaxed activity for child

THE NEXT DAY

- ☐ Discuss party with child
- ☐ Make mental or written notes for the next party
- ☐ Help child send thank-you notes

A Permanent Record of the Party

9/15/64

"Blowing
out
Candles"

9/15/64

"Pin the Button
on the
Clown"

9/15/64

"Parade with hats
and table favors

Harmonicas
given
as prizes"

9/15/64

"Animals
Fly"

I was
saying
"Doggly."

Many families like to have their children's parties recorded in some permanent form. Amateur photography is the most popular method. A simple Brownie-type camera with a flash attachment is all you need to capture the birthday child's expressions. Color film—if within your budget—can be used to advantage.

Most photographs will find their way into family albums or letters to distant relatives. Colored slides and home movies often present a more complete record, which can be run off for the family's enjoyment year after year.

The best setting for photographs is while the children are seated at the table. It is probably the only time when they are all in one place for more than a minute! And their faces seem to be particularly expressive when the candle-lit birthday cake is brought out. Another good opportunity for pictures is during the game period, but care must be exercised not to interfere with the games.

If another member of the family or a friend is present, it is easier to arrange for this person to handle the photography. This leaves you free to continue with the other aspects of the party.

Professional photography is not suggested. The professional photographer tends to want to show each child to his best advantage. The children, after all, have come to the party to enjoy themselves—not to pose over and over again.

If a tape recorder is available, it is amusing to record portions of the games as well as the singing of "Happy Birthday." If the tape recorder can be operated from another room, the children will be less self-conscious. The microphone can be hidden in the room and connected to the tape recorder by an extension cord.

At the end of the party, the tape may be played back for the children, if they are interested. Or it can be edited and saved for family gatherings, when it may be coupled with slides or movies taken at the same party.

Betty Crocker's Party Planner of
MENUS AND RECIPES

The magic ingredients that make a party a grand and glorious success are a gay theme, delicious food, and lively, interesting games. Planning refreshments for young guests is simple when you pick a party from this chapter. You'll find complete menus with recipes and suggested games which will help you carry out the party theme for many special occasions. And to find more delightful party games, consult the guides on pages 28-33.

Backyard Pet Show

What fun! Children have a pet parade. Serve box lunches and Puppy Dog Cake.

GAMES TO PLAY	PAGE
ANIMALS FLY	36
PIN THE TAIL ON THE DONKEY	40
ANIMAL HUNT	65
PIG RACE	81

MENU

Peanut Butter Sandwiches and
Meat Sandwiches (cut in 1″ strips)
Deviled Egg Halves
Carrot and Celery Sticks
Ice Cream
Puppy Dog Cake
Fruit Punch

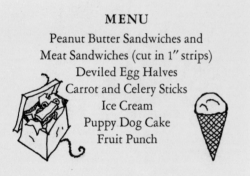

Deviled Egg Halves

6 hard-cooked eggs
½ tsp. salt
¼ tsp. pepper
¼ tsp. dry mustard
about 3 tbsp. salad dressing or cream (enough to moisten)

Cut eggs in halves. Slip out yolks. Mash with fork or electric mixer. Mix in seasonings and salad dressing; continue mashing until smooth. Refill whites with egg-yolk mixture, heaping it lightly. Chill.

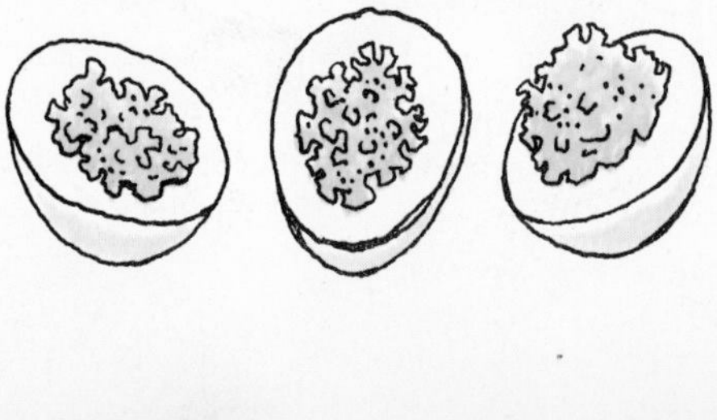

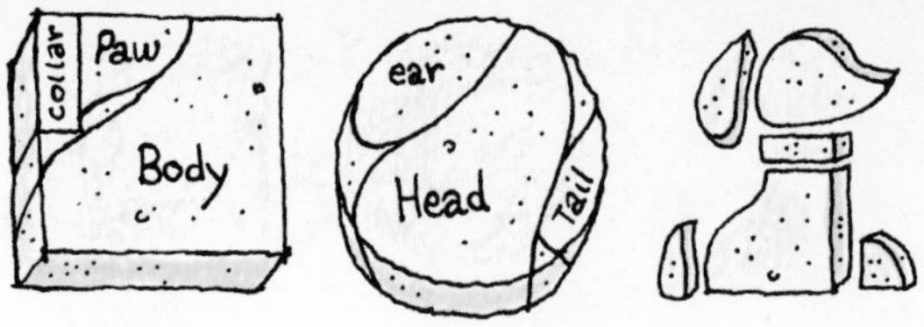

Puppy Dog Cake

Prepare our white, yellow, or devils food cake mix as directed on package except—bake ½ of batter in a square pan, 8 x 8 x 2″, and the remaining batter in a round pan, 8 x 1½″. Cool and remove from pans.

Cut body, paw, and collar from square cake; cut head, tail, and ear from round cake as shown. Arrange cake pieces on a tray (see sketch). Prepare our fluffy white frosting mix as directed on package. Frost entire dog, joining all parts.

Melt 2 sq. semisweet chocolate (2 oz.). With small spatula, spread chocolate over frosting on ears and collar. Draw eyes and mouth with melted chocolate. Outline body parts with pieces of black licorice (see sketch). Give him a gumdrop nose.

Cinderella Supper

A girls' party with "slipper" cutouts for invitations and Magic Pumpkin Cake for dessert.

GAMES TO PLAY	PAGE
TIME!	49
IDENTIFYING MONTHS	108
SHOE SCRAMBLE	129
STUNTS IN MAGIC BOXES	137

MENU

Princess Sandwiches
Fairy Godmother Fruit Salad
Magic Pumpkin Cake
Royal Palace Punch   Milk

Princess Sandwiches

As dainty and feminine as Cinderella herself are finger sandwiches of thinly sliced chicken between slices of lightly buttered dark and light bread.

Fairy Godmother Fruit Salad

Mix pineapple tidbits, banana slices, and mandarin orange sections with sweetened whipped cream. Serve on lettuce.

Magic Pumpkin Cake

Bake our orange chiffon cake mix in 10″ tube pan as directed on package. Prepare our fluffy white frosting mix as directed on package. Reserve ¼ cup frosting; tint with about 5 drops of green food coloring. Tint remaining frosting with ¼ tsp. *each* red and yellow food coloring to make pumpkin color.

Place cake top side up on plate. Frost top, sides, and 1″ down inside center hole with ¼″ of frosting. Spread remaining frosting on upper half of sides and outer half of top; shape round like a pumpkin. Make grooves by pulling tip of spatula through frosting, starting at bottom and bringing up to center. For the stem, insert a peeled banana in hole of cake and spread with reserved green frosting. Serve as soon as possible.

Royal Palace Punch

Serve one of the delicious frozen fruit concentrates, such as pineapple-orange concentrate, diluted with water or ginger ale.

Big Top Birthday Party

Red, white, and blue paper streamers make a circus-tent tablecloth.

MENU
Hot Dogs with "the Works"
Baked Beans in Circus Pot
Carnival Angel Cake
or Carnival Cupcakes
Pink Lemonade   Milk

Carnival Angel Cake

Bake our angel food cake mix as directed on package. When thoroughly cool, remove from pan. Prepare our fluffy white frosting mix and frost cake. Dip 4 animal crackers in melted semisweet chocolate. With knife, mark top and sides of cake into 8 equal wedges. Sprinkle colored decorating candies over alternate wedges. (Put candy in folded waxed paper and tap paper gently to sprinkle candy evenly.) Insert colored birthday candles into 4 large gumdrops. Place on white wedges close to center hole. Rest front feet of chocolate-coated animal crackers on gumdrops and back feet on frosting.

Carnival Cupcakes

Bake cupcakes as directed on any of our layer cake mixes except toffee swirl or marble. Prepare our fluffy white frosting mix as directed on package. Frost cupcakes; sprinkle with colored decorating candies and top with a chocolate-coated animal cracker (above).

Have a Ball! Party

Sports fans everywhere will applaud this special birthday party theme.

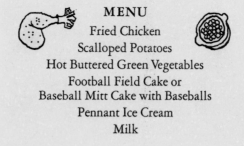

MENU
Fried Chicken
Scalloped Potatoes
Hot Buttered Green Vegetables
Football Field Cake or
Baseball Mitt Cake with Baseballs
Pennant Ice Cream
Milk

Scalloped Potatoes

These are so easy to make with a package of our scalloped potatoes.

Football Field Cake

Prepare our white, yellow, or devils food cake mix as directed on package except—bake in a greased and floured jelly roll pan, 15½ x 10½ x 1", for 20 to 22 min. Turn out of the pan onto large tray or bread board covered with aluminum foil; cool.

Make our chocolate fudge flavor frosting mix as directed on package. Frost top and sides of the cake. Mix 1 cup sifted confectioners' sugar with 2 to 3 tsp. water for decorating icing. Fill a decorating tube with this icing and make the yard and goal lines. The pennants and goal posts can be made with wooden skewers or lollipop sticks. Cut tiny flags from colored construction paper.

Baseball Diamond or Basketball Court Cake: Make cake as directed above except—decorate as baseball diamond or basketball court.

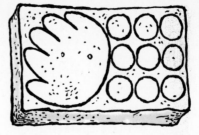

Baseball Mitt Cake

Prepare our yellow cake mix as directed on package except—bake in a greased and floured jelly roll pan, 15½ x 10½ x 1", 20 to 22 min. Cool in the pan 10 min. Remove and finish cooling.

Baseball Mitt: Place right hand on left side of cake and trace around it. Enlarge size of fingers and extend to make mitt about 9½" from fingers to wrist. Cut around outline. Hollow palm of mitt slightly. Prepare our caramel fudge frosting mix as directed on package; frost cake. Cut licorice rope candy into short strips and lay between fingers for laces.

Baseballs: From remaining cake, cut baseballs using 2 to 2½" round cutter. Prepare our creamy white frosting mix as directed on package. Frost tops and sides of baseballs. Fill decorating tube with remainder of frosting used on mitt. Draw stitching lines on baseballs. Place one ball in palm of mitt. Put birthday candles in the other balls and arrange around the mitt.

Pennant Ice Cream

Slice pint bricks of Neapolitan ice cream so that each slice has a stripe of chocolate, vanilla, and strawberry.

Spacemen's Party

A boys' party with space suits and helmets and a trip to the science museum!

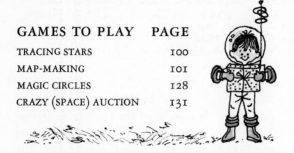

MENU
Sputnik Cheeseburgers
Satellite Tomatoes
Rocket Cake
Saturn Sodas

Sputnik Cheeseburgers

Prepare open-face cheeseburgers. Garnish with pickle slices held in place with colored toothpicks.

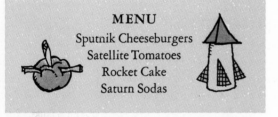

Satellite Tomatoes

Cut small carrots, celery sticks, and green onions the same length, about 3½". Wash medium tomatoes; peel, if desired. To make satellites, remove tomato cores. Make two small slashes about ½" long in each tomato on either side of hole where core was removed. Insert a carrot stick and a celery stick. Insert onion in center of each tomato. Serve as individual salads.

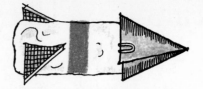

Rocket Cake

Prepare our orange chiffon cake mix as directed on package except—bake batter in an ungreased jelly roll pan, 15½ x 10½ x 1", and in an ungreased loaf pan, 9 x 5 x 3". Bake sheet cake about 20 min.; the loaf, 25 to 30 min. Invert the cakes to cool, using clothespins for legs.

When the sheet cake has cooled about 10 min., loosen sides and ease out of pan onto towel which has been generously dusted with confectioners' sugar. Beginning at short side, roll up the cake. When cool, unroll cake; spread with Sweetened Whipped Cream (below); reroll. Prepare our creamy white frosting mix as directed on package; reserve small amount and tint red. Frost roll white; frost a 1- to 2"-wide red band around the middle of roll. Finish with a shiny nose cone fashioned from heavy-duty aluminum foil. Use sugar wafers or 5" white cardboard triangles for tail fins.

Sweetened Whipped Cream: Beat 1 cup whipping cream, ½ cup sifted confectioners' sugar, and ½ tsp. vanilla in small mixer bowl until stiff enough to hold point.

Saturn Sodas

Since yellow-orange rings surround Saturn, serve a scoop of orange sherbet in each tall glass of cold orange-flavored soft drink.

Faraway Places Party

Ship Ahoy! Anchors Aweigh!—and off we go crossing the seven seas!

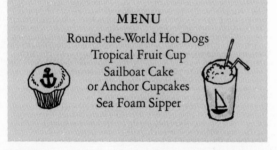

MENU
Round-the-World Hot Dogs
Tropical Fruit Cup
Sailboat Cake
or Anchor Cupcakes
Sea Foam Sipper

Round-the-World Hot Dogs

Serve lots of broiled wieners on hot buttered toasted buns. To give the wieners a Round-the-World taste, serve relishes that come from many places. Explain that the sliced stuffed olives come from Italy, the heated pineapple spears from Hawaii, the mustard from China, the hot chili sauce from Mexico, and so on.

Tropical Fruit Cup

Cut up your choice of fresh or canned fruit—apples, pears, peaches, pineapple—or use canned fruit cocktail combined with diced apple for crunch. Just before serving, pour chilled lemon-lime carbonated beverage over fruit.

Sailboat Cake

Prepare your favorite flavor of our layer cake mixes (other than toffee swirl or marble) as directed on package except—fill a square pan, 9 x 9 x 1¾″, half full of batter and bake 30 to 35 min. Bake remaining batter in muffin pans lined with paper baking cups.

When square cake is cool, cut as shown in the first diagram. (Note that rectangle "A" is slightly larger than "B.") Arrange cake pieces on tray as shown in the second diagram.

Prepare our fluffy white frosting mix as directed on package. Remove ½ of the frosting to another bowl and tint light blue. Frost sail in horizontal blue and white stripes; frost hull of boat blue. (Use remaining frosting for cupcakes.) Add round white candies for portholes on the hull.

Anchor Cupcakes

Serve these and save the Sailboat Cake for a family party later, if you like.

Frost cupcakes with fluffy white frosting. Fill a decorating tube or an envelope with a tiny corner cut off with light blue fluffy frosting; make an anchor on each cupcake. Leave cupcakes in paper cups for easy handling.

Sea Foam Sipper

Serve tall glasses of cold Strawberry or Raspberry Milk (see page 159) topped with whipped cream "sea foam."

May Basket Party

Use a pastel cloth and paper lace doilies; give tiny spring flower corsages to the girls.

MENU
Chickenburgers-in-a-Basket
Carrot Sticks
Basket-of-Flowers Cupcakes
Strawberry or Raspberry Milk

Chickenburgers-in-a-Basket

½ lb. Cheddar cheese, cubed
2 sweet pickles, chopped
2 cups cut-up cooked chicken
1 tsp. grated onion
⅓ cup mayonnaise
10 hamburger buns

Mix cheese, pickles, chicken, onion, and mayonnaise. Season to taste. Split and butter buns. Fill with chicken mixture and replace tops. Wrap in aluminum foil and refrigerate. When ready to serve, heat in 350° (mod.) oven for 15 min. Serve in a doily-lined basket that has a bunch of flowers tied on the handle. *10 servings.*

Basket-of-Flowers Cupcakes

Bake cupcakes as directed on any of our layer cake mixes except toffee swirl or marble. Frost with white or chocolate frosting. Fill a decorating tube with tinted frosting and make roses, violets, buttercups, and green leaves on top of cakes—or shape flowers and leaves of cut-up colored gumdrops. Ribbon-covered wire handles or pipe cleaners transform cakes into baskets of flowers.

Strawberry or Raspberry Milk

cold milk
raspberry or strawberry jam or ice cream topping or thawed frozen berries
red food coloring

For each serving, beat or shake 1 cup milk with 2 heaping tsp. jam, topping, or berries. Add 2 or 3 drops coloring, if desired.

Fourth of July Party

This is the perfect day for a children's parade and a picnic.

GAMES TO PLAY	PAGE
SCAVENGER HUNT	66
PUSH PEANUT RACE	80
STEPPING STONES	97
TRACING STARS	100

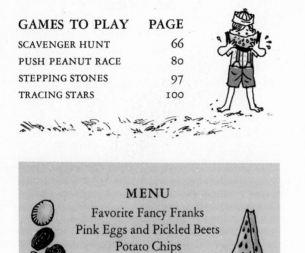

MENU
Favorite Fancy Franks
Pink Eggs and Pickled Beets
Potato Chips
Icy Watermelon Wedges
Brownie S'Mores

Favorite Fancy Franks

Coney Islands: Make Coney Sauce (below). Slit 8 franks diagonally; grill over hot coals until brown. Split 8 frankfurter rolls; butter, then toast (only an instant). Spoon Coney Sauce generously into each frank-filled roll.

Coney Sauce: In saucepan, heat 1 can (1 lb. 4 oz.) chili con carne, 1 can (6 oz.) tomato paste, 1 tsp. prepared mustard, and ½ tsp. salt.

Cheesy Pups: Make biscuit dough as directed on Bisquick package except—add ½ cup grated sharp cheese to dough. Coat hands with Bisquick and pat dough around weiners, making a thin covering. Wrap one strip of bacon around dough, securing with toothpicks. Put on skewers or peeled sticks. Roast over coals until bacon is crisp and dough is baked and lightly browned. *Makes about 12.*

Pink Eggs

These are traditional for a Fourth of July picnic, say some old-timers.

Shell hard-cooked eggs. Place in a bowl with juice drained from a jar of pickled beets. Chill eggs, turning occasionally, until pink on all sides. Remove from beet juice and dry with paper toweling. Serve eggs chilled with salt and pepper. For tart relish, serve the pickled beets.

Brownie S'Mores

Prepare our fudge brownie mix as directed on the package except—bake in a jelly roll pan, 15½ x 10½ x 1", for 15 min. When cool, cut into 48 pieces.

At picnic, place two 1" squares of milk chocolate candy on 24 brownies. Toast 24 marshmallows over hot coals. Slip toasted marshmallow onto chocolate-topped brownie; cover with a plain brownie. *Makes 2 dozen.*

Patriotic Birthday Party

Paper axes for place cards on a red-white-and-blue tablecloth.

GAMES TO PLAY	PAGE
PAPER HUNT	76
HORSE RACE	82
CHIP CHANGE	130
MAGIC BOXES	134

MENU
Baked Ham Slices
Potato Chips
Sweet Pickles
Carrot Sticks
Buttered Rolls
Star Cake
Cold Milk with Peppermint Sticks

Star Cake

Bake our white or yellow cake mix in layer pans, 8 x 1½", as directed on package. Cool. On one layer, space 5 toothpicks 4½" apart around outside edge to mark the star points. About 2½" in from the edge, place 5 more toothpicks, spacing them evenly between every two of the outside toothpicks. Cut out pieces of cake, cutting from the outside to the inside toothpicks to form star points. Frost star and cutout pieces with Glaze (below). Place star in center of serving plate and arrange cake pieces, with rounded sides toward center, around star. Insert small candles in red gumdrop candies; place on cake pieces and star points, depending on number of birthday candles desired.

Glaze: Heat ⅓ cup milk and 1 tbsp. white corn syrup in small saucepan. In small mixer bowl, beat milk mixture and 1 package of our creamy white frosting mix until smooth. Add 1 to 2 tbsp. more milk, if necessary.

Halloween Party

Bob for apples, carve a pumpkin, play spooky games.

MENU
Witches' Cauldron Soup
Goblin Franks
Vegetable Relishes
Ice Cream Jack-O'-Lanterns
Milk   Halloween Cookies

Witches' Cauldron Soup

Serve a simple soup from a large bowl set inside a kettle with a handle which has been covered with black paper. If served in mugs, children can drink broth and spoon out vegetables.

Goblin Franks

1½ cups Gold Medal Flour	¼ tsp. paprika
½ cup corn meal	⅛ tsp. cayenne
1 tsp. baking powder	½ cup shortening
1 tsp. salt	½ to ⅔ cup milk
½ tsp. dry mustard	8 wieners

Heat oven to 450° (hot). In a bowl, stir flour, corn meal, baking powder, and seasonings together. Cut in shortening. Stir in milk just to make a soft dough. Divide dough into two parts. Roll each into a rectangle, about 12 x 6". Cut each rectangle into 4 parts. Place wieners lengthwise on dough, moisten edges of dough, roll up, and seal edges with a fork. Place on baking sheet; sprinkle with paprika. Bake 15 to 20 min., or until lightly browned. Serve as a finger food with a dip of catsup or chili sauce.
Note: When using Gold Medal Self-Rising Flour, omit baking powder and salt.

Ice Cream Jack-O'-Lanterns

At least 24 hours before serving, make firm, well-rounded, large scoops of vanilla ice cream. On one side of scoop, use chocolate bits and slices of cherry to make a jack-o'-lantern face. Freeze uncovered until 10 to 15 min. before serving time. Just before serving, insert a tiny yellow birthday candle in top of jack-o'-lantern. Serve lighted.

Aloha Party

Paper leis, Hawaiian music, fruit punch—for real Island atmosphere.

MENU
Salad Tropicale
Assorted Meat Sandwiches
Sweet Potato Casserole
Coconut Palm Cake
Cold Fruit Punch

Salad Tropicale

Bananas, pineapple, and citrus fruits are a must in a fruit salad for a Hawaiian party. Add melon balls or other fruits according to the season. Serve in dessert dishes or in one of the following special ways.

Melon Bowl for Salad: Fruit salad becomes a conversation piece when served in a hollowed-out watermelon half.

Fruit-filled Pineapple Boats: Cut fresh pineapple in half, leaves and all. Cut out core and fruit, leaving shell about ½″ thick. Serve each guest a pineapple boat filled with Salad Tropicale.

Sweet Potato Casserole

Heat oven to 350° (mod.). Combine 2 cups mashed sweet potatoes, ¼ cup soft butter, and ¾ tsp. salt in a greased 1-qt. baking dish. Sprinkle ½ cup miniature marshmallows over top. Bake uncovered for 20 min., until the marshmallows are lightly browned. *4 to 6 servings.*

Coconut Palm Cake

Bake our white, yellow, or devils food cake mix in layer pans, 8 x 1½″, as directed on the package. When cool, fill and frost with fluffy white frosting prepared from our mix. Sprinkle sides of cake thickly with flaked fresh or canned coconut. On top of the cake, arrange a coconut palm tree using a cinnamon stick or chocolate candy roll as a trunk and slices of green peppermint gumdrops for leaves. Add chocolate candy pieces for coconuts. Place birthday candles in holders around cake.

To Prepare Fresh Coconut: Pierce 2 holes in eyes of coconut. Drain out milk. Place coconut in shallow pan and heat in 350° (mod.) oven for 30 min. Cool. Break the shell with hammer or chisel. With knife, remove coconut meat from shell. Pare off brown skin. Shred white meat. (Keep unused portion in tightly covered jar in refrigerator.)

Skating or Caroling Party

Serve supper around a crackling fire; sing carols.

GAMES TO PLAY	PAGE
HOT, WARM, COLD	47
TWENTY QUESTIONS	55
NEWSPAPER RACE	85
PERSONAL BINGO	104
JINGLE BELLS	149

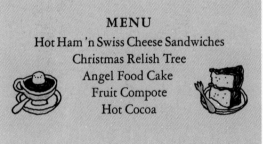

MENU
Hot Ham 'n Swiss Cheese Sandwiches
Christmas Relish Tree
Angel Food Cake
Fruit Compote
Hot Cocoa

Ham 'n Swiss Cheese Sandwiches

Split and butter hamburger buns. Spread one side with prepared mustard and pickle relish, if desired. Insert a slice of baked or boiled ham and a slice of Swiss cheese. Wrap sandwiches in foil; refrigerate. Before serving, place foil-wrapped buns on baking sheet. Heat in 350° (mod.) oven for 20 to 25 min. Serve in foil wrapping from a big basket.

Christmas Relish Tree

Use a three-tiered serving tray or set a small compote atop a footed cake plate. Fill with all sorts of crisp relishes: pickles, stuffed celery, carrot sticks, olives. Top with a tree ornament.

Early Morn' Party

After a hearty breakfast, plan a hike and a scavenger hunt.

GAMES TO PLAY	PAGE
THREE UP	46
SCAVENGER HUNT	66
SCOOP BEAN RACE	85
FEEL IT!	111

MENU
Flapjacks and Syrup
Grilled Canadian Bacon and Sausages
Milk or Cocoa

Flapjacks

Mix thoroughly 1⅔ cups milk or water and 2 cups Bisquick. Drop batter by spoonfuls onto lightly greased, hot skillet. Turn when bubbles appear and the edges begin to dry. *Makes 12 to 14 flapjacks.*

Grilled Canadian Bacon and Sausages

1½ lb. Canadian bacon, unsliced	⅛ tsp. cloves
¼ cup maple-flavored syrup	1 pkg. (8 oz.) brown-and-serve sausages
½ tsp. hickory smoked salt	

With a sharp knife, make ½" deep diagonal cuts at ½" intervals in surface of Canadian bacon. Repeat cuts at an angle to make squares on surface. Mix syrup, salt, and cloves to make a basting sauce. Place Canadian bacon on grill about 3" from coals. Broil 30 to 45 min., turning often and basting with the basting sauce. Add the sausages the last 6 min. and broil until heated through, basting once or twice with sauce. Serve immediately. *About 8 servings.*

Spring Party

Plan an Easter Candy Hunt and an Egg Race. Serve "bunny food" for fun!

MENU
Bunny-shaped Sandwiches
Carrot and Celery Sticks
Easter Bunny Cake
Milk

Easter Egg Party Favors

Egg Heads: Paint faces on empty egg shells (below). Make hair and/or hats with paper lace doilies, yarn, scraps of fabric, anything at hand. Set upright on collar—a 1"-wide strip of cardboard slit up one end and shaped into a ring.

Piglets: Start with colored eggs. Add paper tail and ears; a nose and four legs of gumdrops.

Egg 'n Chick: Cut top off colored empty egg shell, leaving zigzag edge. Fill egg with paper grass. Top grass with fluffy yellow chick from the variety store.

Easter Egg Carton: Cover a cardboard egg carton with purple paper. Stuff each egg space with paper grass as a cushion for twelve decorated eggs.

To Empty Egg Shells: Wash and dry fresh eggs. Prick a hole in both ends of each egg with a needle. Blow egg from shell. If blowing is difficult, enlarge hole with needle. (Refrigerate egg yolk and white immediately for scrambled eggs.) Decorate.

Bunny-shaped Sandwiches

Cut slices of white bread with bunny cooky cutter. Spread with butter. Fill with sliced ham and lettuce trimmed to fit. Add a bit of carrot for bunny's eye. Put slice of carrot in bunny's hand.

Easter Bunny Cake

Bake our white or yellow cake mix in layers as directed on package. When cake is cool, cut one layer in half. Prepare our fluffy white frosting mix as directed on package. Put halves of cake together with frosting or with whipped cream. Stand upright on cut edge. With a sharp knife, cut a notch about a third of the way around the semi-circle to form the rabbit's head (see sketch). Save cutout piece for the tail; secure it in place with a toothpick. Frost rabbit with remaining frosting or whipped cream and cover generously with coconut. Cut ears from white paper; color inside pink with crayon. Color about a teaspoon of frosting or cream pink for the eyes and nose. Coconut tinted green or paper grass and a few Easter eggs form an attractive nest around the bunny.

Patio Party

Play favorite games; cook out on the backyard barbecue grill.

MENU
Double Decker Hamburgers
on Toasted Buns
Roasted Ears of Corn
Sliced Fresh Tomatoes
Jack Horner Prune Cake
Milk or Lemonade

Double Decker Hamburgers

2 lb. ground beef	dash of pepper
2 eggs	½ cup bread crumbs
2 tsp. salt	

Mix all ingredients; shape into 16 thin hamburger patties. On ½ the patties, spread one or more fillings (below); top with remaining patties and seal edges. Place on grill 4 to 6″ from hot coals or put in squares of heavy-duty aluminum foil and place directly on top of coals. Cook 15 to 20 min., or until done as desired. Serve on toasted hamburger buns. *Makes 8 hamburgers.*

Fillings to Mix and Match: Dill pickles slices, pickle relish, prepared mustard, catsup, horseradish, chopped onions, onion slices, Cheddar cheese slices, pasteurized cheese spread.

Onion Filling: Mix 1 package (1½ oz.) dehydrated onion soup mix with ¼ cup water.

Peppy Cheese Filling: Mix 2 oz. shredded Cheddar cheese with 1 tsp. salt, ¼ tsp. pepper, 2 tbsp. mayonnaise, 1 tsp. Worcestershire sauce, and ½ tsp. mustard.

Jack Horner Prune Cake

1 cup boiling water	1¼ tsp. soda
1 cup cut-up, pitted uncooked prunes	1 tsp. *each* cinnamon, nutmeg, cloves
2 cups Gold Medal Flour	½ cup vegetable oil
1½ cups sugar	3 eggs (½ to ⅔ cup)
1 tsp. salt	1 cup chopped nuts

Pour boiling water over cut-up prunes. Let stand for 2 hr. Heat oven to 350° (mod.). Grease and flour an oblong pan, 13 x 9½ x 2″. In large mixer bowl, stir dry ingredients together; add prune mixture and all other ingredients. Blend thoroughly (about 1 min.). Beat 2 min. medium speed on mixer or 300 strokes by hand. Pour into prepared pan. Bake 45 to 50 min., or until the cake tests done. Cool in pan; frost with Orange Butter Icing (below).

Orange Butter Icing: Blend ⅓ cup soft butter and 3 cups sifted confectioners' sugar. Stir in 3 tbsp. orange juice until smooth. Blend in 1½ tbsp. grated orange rind.

Best Birthday Cakes

For a beautiful birthday cake—traditional style—mix or match these favorite cakes and frostings. Trim with colorful birthday candles and, if you like, add mints, gumdrops, marshmallows, peppermint sticks, or other candy. Or use the special candle holders described below.

Devils Food Birthday Cake

1⅔ cups Gold Medal Flour	½ cup cocoa
1½ cups sugar	½ cup soft shortening
1¼ tsp. soda	1 cup milk
1 tsp. salt	1 tsp. vanilla
	3 eggs (½ to ⅔ cup)

Heat oven to 350° (mod.). Grease and flour two layer pans, 8 or 9 x 1½", or an oblong pan, 13 x 9½ x 2". In large mixer bowl, stir together dry ingredients; add shortening, milk, and vanilla. Blend thoroughly (about 1 min.). Beat 2 min. medium speed on mixer or 300 strokes by hand. Scrape sides and bottom of bowl constantly. Add eggs. Beat 2 min., scraping bowl frequently. Pour into prepared pans. Bake 8" layers 38 min., 9" layers 30 min., oblong 45 min., or until cake tests done. Cool; frost.

Starlight Birthday Cake

2 cups plus 2 tbsp. Gold Medal Flour	½ cup soft shortening
1½ cups sugar	1 cup milk
3½ tsp. baking powder	1 tsp. vanilla
1 tsp. salt	3 eggs (½ to ⅔ cup)

Heat oven to 350° (mod.). Grease and flour two layer pans, 8 or 9 x 1½", or an oblong pan, 13 x 9½ x 2". In large mixer bowl, stir together dry ingredients; add shortening, milk, and vanilla. Blend thoroughly (about 1 min.). Beat 2 min. medium speed on mixer or 300 strokes by hand. Scrape sides and bottom of bowl constantly. Add eggs. Beat 2 min., scraping bowl frequently. Pour into prepared pans. Bake 8" layers 35 to 40 min., 9" layers 30 to 35 min., oblong 45 to 50 min., or until cake tests done. Cool; frost.

Creamy Chocolate Frosting

2½ cups confectioners' sugar	3 sq. unsweetened chocolate (3 oz.), melted
¾ cup Gold Medal Flour	1 tsp. vanilla
¼ tsp. salt	1 tbsp. light corn syrup
⅓ cup soft butter	⅓ cup milk

Blend all ingredients together and stir until smooth. If necessary, gradually stir in 2 tbsp. milk to make a good spreading consistency.

Double Boiler Frosting

FOR LAYER CAKES	FOR OBLONG CAKE
2 egg whites (¼ cup)	1 egg white (2 tbsp.)
1½ cups sugar	¾ cup sugar
¼ tsp. cream of tartar or 1 tbsp. light corn syrup	⅛ tsp. cream of tartar or 1½ tsp. light corn syrup
⅓ cup water	3 tbsp. water
1 tsp. vanilla	½ tsp. vanilla

Mix all ingredients except vanilla in top of double boiler. Place over boiling water; beat with rotary beater until stiff peaks form. Scrape bottom and sides of pan occasionally. Fold in vanilla.

Special Birthday Candle Holders

Candle Rings: Place each birthday candle in a hard candy circle (11 to a roll) on frosted cake.

Flower Pastels: Place each birthday candle in the center of a circle of 5 colored miniature marshmallows on frosted cake. Use marshmallows of the same color for each circle.

Cheery Cherries: Press each birthday candle into the hole of stem end of red or green maraschino cherry. Place on frosted cake.

Index

Games

Games (Continued)

Recipes